NEW OXFORD ENGLISH

1

Anne Powling

John O'Connor

Geoff Barton

Oxford University Press

INTRODUCTION

New Oxford English has been devised to introduce you to every aspect of the new National Curriculum in English through enjoyable, stimulating activities and resources which are exciting and attractive to use. *Students' Books 1–3* are designed for use in Key Stage 3, or Years S1 and S2 in Scotland.

The four modules

Each book is divided into four sections, or 'modules', which reflect four major areas of work in the English classroom: Narrative, Poetry, Non-Fiction and Drama.

- In the **Narrative** modules you will learn about the many different ways in which stories are told, both through speech and writing, and look at a wide variety of narrative forms.
- The **Poetry** modules ask you to do everything from performing a poem to creating your own 'newspaper poetry', and offer a range of poems from writers as different as Judith Nicholls, Benjamin Zephaniah, and Robert Southey.
- **Non-Fiction** includes everything from advertisements to encyclopedias; and in these modules you will have the opportunity to explore media, such as television and CD-ROM, as well as printed materials, such as information books and leaflets.
- In the **Drama** modules you will learn how to write and perform plays, as well as how to get the most out of those that other people have written; and you will be introduced to radio scripts and 'screen-plays', as well as plays written for the stage.

You can find full details of the range of extracts in *New Oxford English Book 1* on page 159 and see how it covers the National Curriculum Programmes of Study on page 3.

Language Study

After each module there is a Language Study unit, which deals with features of language work (such as grammar, punctuation, or the study of dialect) which have arisen from that particular module. For example, the Poetry module contains a poem called *Wordhunter's Collection* and this leads on to work in the Language Study unit on where words come from, and how many are borrowed from other languages.

Using New Oxford English

You are not expected to work in any set order through the modules in each book: you might be performing a play one day and discussing advertisements on the video the next. It is helpful, though, to link the features in the Language Study units with the modules to which they are attached. In that way, language work can arise naturally from the texts you are looking at or the activities you are engaged in.

Taking it further

These extension activities together with photocopiable sheets from the Teacher's Book will give you the opportunity to continue work you have particularly enjoyed and to develop your skills in English.

The video

A video accompanies each Students' Book and this permits you, for example, to see a storyteller at work, think about excerpts from television serials, discuss advertisements, watch actors performing their roles in different ways, and compare you own performances with other students'.

We hope that you will enjoy using and viewing New Oxford English.

New Oxford English 1 and the National Curriculum

PROGRAMMES OF STUDY	MODULE 1 NARRATIVE	MODULE 2 POETRY	MODULE 3 NON-FICTION	MODULE 4 DRAMA
Speaking and Listening				
1a Talking for different purposes	Telling Your Own Stories A Chain of Events	Puzzling Word Pictures	Looking at Reading Habits Instructions • Recipe Cards	Inventing a Story • Focusing on Story and Character
1b Talking in a range of contexts	A Chain of Events • Spotting the Pattern • Deciding on the Right Punctuation	Cautionary Tales Pictures in Writing	Hazard House The Knowledge Challenge Holiday Ahoy	Building Characters Reading a Script Punctuating Dialogue
1c Listening attentively	A Chain of Events Different Versions	Cautionary Tales Experimenting with Sound	Instructions • Hazard House Holiday Ahoy • Simply Take	Inventing a Story Reading a Script
1d Drama, role play, and performance	Different Versions	Cautionary Tales Reading the Whole Story	Holiday Challenge	Inventing a Story • Reading a Script • Shakespeare and Stage Directions
2a Structuring and adapting talk	Telling Your Own Stories A Chain of Events	Cautionary Tales Shaping Stories	Instructions • Hazard House Holiday Challenge	Building Characters
2b Effective listening and responding	Features of Science Fiction	Cautionary Tales Pictures in Writing	Instructions • Hazard House Holiday Ahoy • Simply Take	Reading a Script
3a Using Standard English fluently and appropriately	A Chain of Events Different Versions	Cautionary Tales Reading the Whole Story	Simply Take	Reading a Script Shakespeare and Stage Directions
3b Development of the language		Where English Words Come From	Different Dialects	Accent • How the Language has Changed
Reading				
1a Reading widely and independently	Creation Myths Features of Science Fiction	A World of Sound The Shape of Poetry	More Than Meets the Eye Turning Points	Focusing on Story and Character Reading a Script
1b Experiencing a variety of genres	A Chain of Events Creation Myths Features of Science Fiction	Reading the Whole Story Pictures in Writing The Shape of Poetry	Instructions •The Knowledge Challenge • More Than Meets the Eye • Recipe Cards	Focusing on Story and Character Reading a Script Setting Out a Script
1c Reading texts from different cultures	Creation Myths	Pictures in Writing Puzzling Word Pictures	Turning Points	
1d Reading works from the literary heritage	Features of Science Fiction	Reading the Whole Story Similes and Metaphors Experimenting with Sound	Turning Points	Focusing on Story and Character Shaping the Play • Shakespeare and Stage Directions
1e Reading non-fiction texts	Spotting the Pattern		Instructions •The Knowledge Challenge • Holiday Ahoy Recipe Cards •Turning Points	
1f Appreciating a range of media	Features of Science Fiction Spotting the Pattern	Pictures in Writing	The Knowledge Challenge Holiday Ahoy • Simply Take	Reading a Script
2a Reading for deeper meanings	Different Versions Adventure on Venda	Pictures in Writing • Picture Poems • Shaping Stories	Looking at Reading Habits Holiday Ahoy • Simply Take	Building Characters Giving Helpful Information
2b Developing informed views on reading	A Chain of Events • Different Versions • Spotting the Pattern	Reading the Whole Story A World of Sound	Looking at Reading Habits Turning Points	Focusing on Story and Character Reading a Script
2c Sifting and evaluating non-fiction texts	Spotting the Pattern		The Knowledge Challenge Holiday Ahoy More Than Meets the Eye	
3a Recognizing features of different types of text	Creation Myths • Two Endings Features of Science Fiction	Reading the Whole Story Picture Poems	Instructions • Holiday Ahoy Simply Take • Turning Points	Building Characters • Focusing on Story and Character
3b Literary language and use of language in non-fiction		Personification • Similes and Metaphors • Sounds Strange Adverbs	Instructions Hazard House	Giving Helpful Information Choosing the Language Verbs and Tenses
Writing				
1a Developing written style	A Lot of Huff and Puff Adventure on Venda	Personification Shaping Stories	Hazard House • Turning Points • About Sentences	Shaping the Play Punctuating Dialogue
1b Writing for different purposes and audiences	Telling Your Own Stories A Lot of Huff and Puff	Drafting a Story Poem Picture Poems	Leaflet Watch More Than Meets the Eye	Giving Helpful Information
1c Writing in a variety of forms	Two Endings A Lot of Huff and Puff Adventure on Venda	Drafting a Story Poem Personification • Picture Poems • Shaping Stories	Instructions • Holiday Challenge • More Than Meets the Eye • Recipe Cards	Shaping the Play Setting Out a Script Punctuating Dialogue
2a Planning, drafting, and presentation	Two Endings Adventure on Venda	Drafting a Story Poem Shaping Stories	Holiday Challenge More Than Meets the Eye	Setting Out a Script
2b Displaying knowledge of text features in own writing	Two Endings Adventure on Venda	Picture Poems Shaping Stories	Instructions Recipe Cards Turning Points	Setting Out a Script Giving Helpful Information
2c Increasing spelling knowledge	Proper Nouns	Verbs Adverbs		Apostrophes • How the Language has Changed
2d Using neat, legible handwriting		Drafting a Story Poem	More Than Meets the Eye	
3a Writing in Standard English and developing knowledge of register	Two Endings Adventure on Venda	Drafting a Story Poem Shaping Stories	More Than Meets the Eye Different Dialects	Shaping the Play Setting Out a Script Giving Helpful Information
3b Understanding sentence level grammar and whole text organisation	Proper Nouns • Sentences and their Punctuation •Statements, Questions, etc. • Commas	Nouns Verbs Adverbs	Paragraphs About Sentences Adjectives	Verbs and Tenses Apostrophes Punctuating Dialogue
3c Using reference texts for extending vocabulary		Verbs • Where English Words Come From		

CONTENTS

MODULE 1 NARRATIVE

MODULE 2 POETRY

CONTENTS

MODULE 3 NON-FICTION

MODULE 4 DRAMA

Telling the Tale
Telling Your Own Stories

Everyday stories

All around us there are stories: news items, gossip, a good joke, the story in an advertisement, or the latest soap. However, the stories we tell most frequently are stories about ourselves.

If someone gave you ten minutes to tell them about the 'real' you, what and who would you talk about? Where would you start? Would you tell your story in a particular order?

This collage is a story in words and pictures of the life of a twelve-year-old girl. She has used photographs, pictures from magazines, news cuttings, her own writing and leaflets to answer the question 'Who am I?'

Here is an explanation of the piece. On your own, look closely at the collage on page 7 and then read Kelly's explanation.

Kelly Bright: Who am I?

I'll start with the man's face, he had such a brilliant expression, a mixture of kindness, experience, energy and he looked enthusiastic about life – all of these are things I'd like to have, or grow to have. I'd like to meet him. I wanted the colours yellow and green in this, yellow for warmth and happiness which I think I have, and green for thinking and relaxing which leads me into the cat and the cushion. For me, these mean curling up warm and comfortable and feeling secure. My own cat does this with me.

I chose the killer whale because it's majestic and free and wild, and independent like the women in the baseball film 'A League of Their Own'. This is my favourite film because it shows women getting up and fighting for what they want which is great.

I had to have a pair of Doc Martins because I love walking on hikes and sponsored walks and they're like an extension of my legs- a uniform I guess.

I chose 'Forever Friends' because friends are so important to keep you happy, while the Nemesis Ride is on there for the thrills and excitement that are important too. I wanted the song lyrics because travel is an ambition and I want to see as much of the world as possible but home is important too which is why I put in the picture of me at Christmas, which for us is a special family time.

Finally in the middle is my cartoon of me. I like drawing cartoons but this shows me as a 'learner' still learning about lots of things. It also sums up my enjoyment of driving my dad's car which he lets me do. The notes represent the keyboard I'm learning.

And that's it!

Who am I?

1 Create your own personal story using a wide range of materials, as Kelly has. As you are making the collage, consider what order you would use to tell someone else your story.

2 Share your picture story with a partner who you do not know very well. Take it in turns to explain the images and words, answering questions and relating the personal stories behind your design.

A Chain Of Events

The Great Escape

Creating the chain

On the previous page you looked at individual important moments but most stories are made up of a sequence of incidents... a chain of events.

The picture story below captures key moments in a hair-raising escape, involving police and a convict from the moment of his escape to his final capture. The pictures are muddled up and it is your job to recreate the story.

In a group of four, arrange the incidents in a logical order with one scene leading to another. Use the scenery and other details in the pictures as clues. The first and last pictures have been left in place to help you.

Philippe Dupasquier

Oral storytelling

Now, in the tradition of the first storytellers you are going to tell your version of the story.

1   Imagine you are the convict describing what happened to your fellow inmates when you are back in the cell.

■ Allocate a certain number of pictures to each person in the group. You will be teller of the story in your pictures.

■ Decide as a group on the personality of the convict, so you all tell the story in the same way. Is he a joker? Does he exaggerate what happened?

■ Begin the process by each person describing events in their pictures and how they feel.

■ Second time round try including more detail: the voices of other characters, sound effects, and your feelings as the convict.

■ If people are uninspired and struggling, offer advice and suggestions.

■ Rehearse once more and then each group can tell their dramatic story to the class.

2   When each group has told its tale, discuss as a class what you think makes a good storyteller. Use examples of people's techniques from the convict story. Draft a series of guidelines to help inspire a nervous storyteller.
Arrange them in order of importance, deciding why you feel one point is more important than another.

From Telling to Writing
Creation Myths

What are the ingredients?

Many of the earliest stories were told to explain how the world came to be as it is: what caused thunder, why winter follows summer, why night follows day. Among these stories are some that explain certain animals' features and why they behave as they do.

Some of the typical ingredients of these creation stories are:

- the involvement of gods and goddesses
- characters who are very good
- characters who are very bad
- characters who learn from experience
- punishments and/or rewards
- supernatural events
- an explanation as to why an animal behaves/looks as it does

1 As a class, listen to the following North American legend about 'How the rattlesnake became' and then individually see how many of the ingredients you can identify.

2 Watch the video clip of a storyteller's version of the African tale, 'How the tortoise got its shell'. How are its ingredients different from *The Great Rain*?

The Great Rain

It was very strange weather. Purple and black clouds raced and tumbled across the sky. They hid the sun, they hid the mountain tops. Inside the clouds lightning flashed and thunder rumbled. Nokomis, the Great Earth Spirit, watched the sky and was worried.

'This isn't the right weather for summer,' she thought. 'Why is the Thunderbird making it so dark and stormy? Thunderbird!' she called. 'What's wrong?'

'Kaaa!' screeched a voice inside the clouds. 'I'll tell you what's wrong! I'm angry!'

There was a flash of lightning and the clouds tore apart.

Nokomis could see the Thunderbird crouching over the mountains, his talons gripping their tops, his open wings stretching from horizon to horizon.

'Very angry!' he shouted, and lightning darted from his red eyes.

'But why are you angry?' asked Nokomis.

'Why?' he glared down at her stretching his neck and rattling his wings to send thunder rolling about the sky.

'I'm angry because the people love you and they don't love me!'

'They love me because I'm the earth, their home,' Nokomis said. 'I'm the rivers where they fish, the forests where they hunt and the plains where they pitch their

teepees. They dance and give thanks to you for the rain that you send,' she reminded him.

'But they love you best!' He beat his wings until the thunder shook the mountainside.

'I'll show them. I'll send them so much rain that the rivers will flood and cover their forests and their plains and their teepees. Everyone will drown. Then they'll be sorry! Kaaa!' He screamed, stretching wide his eagle beak, then pulled the black clouds over himself again.

'Thunderbird, Thunderbird,' called Nokomis, but he would not answer.

Nokomis was very worried. 'What am I going to do?' she thought. 'He won't talk to me. And he won't change his mind. I know him. He'll just sulk up there getting angrier and angrier until he's ready to burst. Then he'll do what he said – make it rain and rain.'

She looked at the mountain where Thunderbird was hiding and thought hard.

'I don't think he can make enough rain to cover everything. Not everything. Not the mountains. Yes! That's it!'

Nokomis called, 'Listen to me, all you animals and people, there is going to be a terrible flood. You must go high up in the mountains, you'll be safe there. You must go quickly.'

Her voice travelled everywhere. In the grass jackrabbits heard her and stopped nibbling. Beneath the ground moles heard her and stopped digging. Under the water beavers heard her and stopped building their dams. Soon all the animals and insects were flying, running, and hopping to the mountains.

It was only the people who took no notice. In their villages they went on sewing moccasins, making arrows and looking at the sky.

Nokomis was puzzled. 'These humans only seem to understand their own language. I must find some other way to warn them, something they will understand.'

She frowned up at the sky. It was much darker and behind the clouds thunder muttered. Soon the Thunderbird would start the rain....

...A little while later an old woman strode into a village. She was tall and thin. Her face and hands were wrinkled like bark. She wore a dress of soft green buckskin with fringes down the sleeves and brown moccasins embroidered with flowers. Her grey hair hung in a long plait and in her headband was one eagle feather dyed red.

Gathering all the people round her, she said, 'The

Thunderbird is very angry. He is going to make so much rain that all this land will be covered with water. If you stay here you will drown, but in the mountains you will be safe.

No one in the village had seen the old woman before, but her face and eyes were very old and very wise so they believed her. They folded their teepees, stamped out their cooking fires, packed pots and blankets and babies into carrying baskets, and went into the mountains.

All that day the old woman hurried from village to village warning people. Soon almost all the people were safe in the mountains. There was only one village left to tell.

As the old woman came near she heard drumming and singing. The people were having a feast. In the centre of the teepees people were dancing, stamping their feet, and jumping high into the air. Some had drums and others had rattles made from dried seed pods and shells tied on to sticks. The noise was louder than the thunder.

No one noticed the old woman come into the village. She called to the dancers, 'Listen to me people!' but they danced on. 'If those drums stopped they could hear me,' she said, but the drummers said, 'This is dancing time Grandma,' and drummed louder.

'Maybe just one person will listen,' she thought. She tried to grab a man dancing by. He pulled his arm away and yelled at her, 'Leave me alone, old woman! Can't you see I'm dancing!'

The old woman was getting angry. She pushed her way through the dancers. She was very strong for such an old woman. She stood in the centre of the dancers and shouted.

'A terrible storm is coming. The water will cover the tops of the tallest trees.'

The people only laughed. 'That will be very wet indeed old woman!' You had better run away quickly or you will be drowned.'

'If you don't go to the mountains it is you who will be drowned,' said the old woman. 'Look at the sky, see how angry the Thunderbird is.'

The sky was full of red and black clouds.

'How does an old woman like you know what the Thunderbird is feeling? Go away!' they shouted. 'You are spoiling our dancing.'

They made a circle and twisted and turned around her, singing and laughing. When she tried to speak again they shook their rattles at her. They pushed her and bumped her.

They were making so much noise that they didn't hear the Thunderbird leap into the air and fly.

'Kaaa!' he screamed. 'Kaaa!'

When thunder boomed and roared from his wings they only shook their rattles and shouted louder than ever.

When the lightning crackled and jumped they leapt higher and shouted, 'See! See! The lightning is dancing with us!'

Even when the rain began to fall, faster and faster, in bigger and bigger drops, they only danced wilder than ever. They whirled and pranced, spinning and kicking.

The old woman watched them. Suddenly she raised her arms and shouted. Her voice was louder than the thunder. It was like a great wind tearing up trees and blowing down mountains.

The dancers and drummers froze. They looked at her with wide-open eyes and mouths.

'So you only want to dance and shake your rattles, eh?' she said. 'You deserve to drown, all of you! But I am Nokomis your Mother, so I will save you. But I will also change you. From this day you will always carry your rattles and whenever you see a human you will dance and shake them. Just as you did today to an old woman who tried to help you.'

As Nokomis spoke, the people began to shrink. They grew smaller and thinner then they began to curl over and crumple. Soon there was no longer a circle of dancers round her but a circle of snakes.

'Now I must take you all to the mountains,' she said, piling them into a large basket.

It rained for days and weeks. Just as the Thunderbird had threatened, the forest and the plain were covered with water. But up in the mountains the animals and the people were safe.

When the rain stopped the water drained away. Soon everybody went back to their homes.

Including the snakes. They went far away from the rain and lived in dry places. And whenever they see a human they raise their heads, sway as if they were dancing, and shake their rattles which they carry in their tails.

And that is how Nokomis the Great Earth Spirit brought rattlesnakes into the world.

Linda Coterill

And They Lived Happily Ever After...

Unlike many folk and fairy tales, myths do not always end happily. The final outcome of a story often depends on the way the characters have behaved during the tale.

Read this summary of the Inuit myth of Sedna which tells 'How the whales and seals became'.

The Ten Fingers Of Sedna

Sedna is a vain girl who teases the men to ask for her hand in marriage. But, when an apparently rich and very handsome man appears she runs away with him, leaving her father alone.

The 'man', however, is actually a bird spirit and she is forced to live on his rocky crag where she pines until her father comes to rescue her. As they escape by boat, the bird spirit implores her not to leave him, protesting his love.

She refuses and the sea begins to rage, threatening the two people in the boat. As the bird vanishes Sedna blames her father for coming to rescue her and he blames her for leaving her husband.

Explaining the ending

The end of the story is on page 15. As you read, consider these questions.

1 Why are the two characters punished?
2 Can you think of the titles of other stories where the characters receive a punishment?
3 What are some of the other reasons for characters in fairy/folk tales, and myths being punished?

As the boat heaved up and down and whirled round in circles, as the lightning flashed and the thunder roared, the two of them fought in the tiny boat. At one point it seemed that Sedna might win, for she was the taller and the stronger of the two, but then somehow her father's thumb found her eye. There was another crash of thunder. Blood poured down her cheek. She staggered backwards and fell overboard.

But still she clung onto the edge of the boat, desperately trying to pull herself back in. With an insane laugh, the father seized his ivory axe. With the wind racing around him, he held it high above his head, then brought it hurtling down. It severed five of Sedna's fingers.

Sedna screamed.

The fingers fell into the foaming sea and turned into seals.

The father struck again with the axe.

Sedna screamed a second time.

The five fingers of her other hand fell into the water and became whales. Sedna disappeared beneath the surface.

The storm died down and the sea grew calm. Unable to go any further, the father turned the boat in towards the shore and pitched his tent on a rocky outcrop on the edge of the beach. He knew that he had done wrong but he was too exhausted and too glad to be alive. Almost at once he fell into a deep sleep

That night there was an unusually high tide. The water came in further than it had ever done before, further than it has ever done since. It came in so far, in fact, that the old man drowned in his sleep. And as the waves lapped over one another, you could almost imagine that the sound they made was the sound of laughter.

A. Horowitz

Two Endings

The reasons why

Below are the endings to two animal creation myths.

1 Read **A** and **B** and then consider which characters are being dealt a happy ending and which an unhappy one. Also ask yourself why you think this is.

2 Working in a pair and sharing ideas, record your answers in a chart like this. The box already completed considers the myth of Sedna to show you how to tackle this activity.

Title The Ten Fingers of Sedna

Why is the character rewarded/punished?

For her vanity first by having to live on the crag.
She is then punished for leaving her husband and for her ingratitude to her father.
The father is punished for killing his daughter.

What kind of reward/punishment do they get?

She becomes the sea goddess.
She loses her fingers: they become seals and whales.
She also loses one eye in the fight with her father and is drowned.
Her father is drowned as he sleeps.

Title How the Elephant Became

Why is the character rewarded/punished?

A ▶ *How the Elephant Became*

Elephant is very unhappy because he cannot discover what he is meant to be. He is too slow and too clumsy, with a big nose and awkward ears. When the animals laugh at him as he rolls in the dust, he goes to an island to live by himself. One night a terrible fire breaks out, fanned by the wind. The animals are trapped on the edge of the river, but the elephant, on his island, is safe. Without pausing, he uses his nose to squirt himself and pick up the animals. Then he uses his tusks to clear trees on the edge of the island to protect them. Next morning, the animals are safe but the elephant has vanished.

'He is still very hard to find. Though he is huge and strong, he is very quiet.

'But what did become of him in the end? Where is he now?

'Ask any of the animals, and they will tell you: "though he is shy, he is the strongest, the cleverest, and the kindest of all the animals. He can carry anything and he can push anything down. He can pick you up in his nose and wave you in the air. We would make him our King if we could get him to wear a crown."'

Ted Hughes

How Crab Got Its Back

In a village lived two very different sisters. One, Esmeralda, was kind, helpful, hard-working, but very plain. The elder, Yolanda, was beautiful, proud, haughty, and lazy. Esmeralda went to the river and met an old woman. The old woman implored her to scratch her back for her and Esmeralda did so. In reward, the woman made her beautiful. Yolanda, jealous of her sister's new beauty, ran to the river to ask for wealth. There the old woman made the same request and she pushed her out of the way, telling her to scratch her own back.

'Insolent girl!' said the old woman. 'As you see *me* so shall *you* be!'

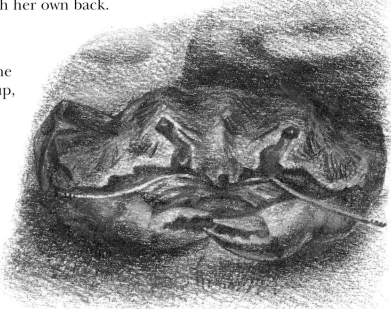

And at that moment Yolanda became an ugly creature, her limbs shrivelled up, turned into her claws, and her back became hard and cracked all over.

She cannot now bear to be seen, for she remembers that once she was beautiful. So she wallows in the mud and hides away under rocks and cliffs. And when sand and mud fill the cracks and her back itches, she rushes down to the river to wash it off for no one will scratch her back.

Grace Hallworth

Writing your own creation myth

You have considered the main ingredients of animal creation myths and looked at possible endings. Now try to write your own. It does not have to be long, but it should explain how your chosen animal came to have its distinctive features.

1   To start with, work with a partner and make a list of animals with distinctive features, calls, or ways of moving.

    e.g. Whale: size and its spout of water
          Zebra: its stripes
          Spider: the way they catch their prey and the number of legs
          Gibbon: the whooping sound of its call

2   Each choose one animal from your list to work with. Between you, decide how they might have come to be.

3   Then on your own, reread your list of ingredients, look at your endings chart, and try writing your own myth.

There is another creation myth on page 40.

Rewriting Stories
Different Versions

Three little pigs

The French fairy story of *The Wolf and The Three Little Pigs* has been shared by parents and children for many years.

1   In pairs, decide who will be **A** and who **B**. **A** should then tell **B** their version of the story of *The Three Little Pigs*. **B** may help if **A** gets stuck at any point.

2   If asked by your teacher, **B** can then relate his/her story to the rest of the class. See how many different versions the class comes up with. Making such changes in retellings is not unusual.

The original story was passed by word of mouth and the teller would often change it to suit the audience. While entertaining, the story was often offered as a warning to young children on the dangers of strangers.

It's all in the telling

This unit features two retellings of *The Three Little Pigs* story.

The first is by a toddler called William. At three points in the story, you are going to be asked about him, his story, and what you think will happen next. With your partner, use the clues in each extract to help you as you read.

William's Version

Part 1

William and Granny were left to entertain each other for an hour while William's mother went to the clinic.

'Sing to me,' said William.

'Granny's too old to sing,' said Granny.

'I'll sing to you, then,' said William. William only knew one song. He had forgotten the words and the tune, but he sang it several times, anyway.

'Shall we do something else now? said Granny.

'Tell me a story,' said William. 'Tell me about the wolf.'

'Red Riding Hood?'

No, not that wolf, the other wolf.'

Peter and the wolf? said Granny.

'Mummy's going to have a baby,' said William.

'I know,' said Granny.

William looked suspicious.

'How do you know?'

'Well... she told me. And it shows, doesn't it?'

'The lady down the road had a baby. It looks like a pig,' said William. He counted on his fingers. 'Three babies looks like three little pigs.

'Ah,' said Granny. 'Once upon a time there were three little pigs. Their names were –'

'They didn't have names,' said William.

'Yes they did. The first pig was called –'

'Pigs don't have names,' said William.

'Some do. These pigs had names.'

'No they didn't.' William slid off Granny's lap and went to open the corner cupboard by the fireplace. Old magazines cascaded out as old magazines do when they have been flung into a cupboard and the door slammed shut. He rooted among them until he found a little book covered with brown paper, climbed into the cupboard, opened the book, closed it and climbed out again.

'They don't have names,' he said.

'I didn't know you could read,' said Granny, properly impressed.

'C – A – T, wheelbarrow,' said William.

'Is that the book Mummy reads to you out of?'

'It's my book,' said William.

'But it's the one Mummy reads.'

'If she says please,' said William.

'Well, that's Mummy's story, then. My pigs have names.'

'They're the wrong pigs.' William was not open to negotiation.

'I don't want them in this story.'

'Can't we have different pigs this time?'

'No. They won't know what to do.'

'Once upon a time,' said Granny, 'there were three little pigs who lived with their mother.'

'Their mother was dead,' said William.

'Oh, I'm sure she wasn't,' said Granny.

'She was dead. You make bacon out of dead pigs. She got eaten for breakfast and they threw the rind out for the birds.'

'So the three little pigs had to find homes for themselves.'

'No.' William consulted his book. 'They had to build little houses.'

'I'm just coming to that.'

'You said they had to find homes. They didn't find them.'

'The first little pig walked along for a bit until he met a man with a load of hay.'

'It was a lady.'

'A lady with a load of hay?'

'NO! It was a lady pig. You said he.'

'I thought all the pigs were little boy-pigs,' said Granny.

'It says lady pig here,' said William. 'It says the lady-pig went for a walk and met a man with a load of hay.'

'So the lady-pig,' said Granny, 'said to the man, "May I have some of that hay to build a house?" and the man said, "Yes." Is that right?'

'Yes,' said William. 'You know that baby?'

'What baby?'

'They one Mummy's going to have. Will that baby have shoes on when it comes out?'

'I don't think so,' said Granny.

'It will have cold feet,' said William.

'Oh, no,' said Granny. 'Mummy will wrap it up in a soft shawl, all snug.'

'I don't mind if it has cold feet,' William explained. 'Go on about the lady-pig.'

'So the lady-pig took the hay and built a little house. Soon the wolf came along and the wolf said –'

'You didn't tell where the wolf lived.'

'I don't know where the wolf lived.'

'15 Tennyson Avenue, next to the bomb-site,' said William.

'I bet it doesn't say that in the book,' said Granny, with spirit.

'Yes it does.'

'Let me see, then,'

William folded himself up with his back to Granny, and pushed the book up under his pullover.

'I don't think it says that in the book,' said Granny.

'It's in ever so small words,' said William.

'So the wolf said, "Little pig, little pig, let me come in," and the little pig answered, "No." So the wolf said, "Then I'll huff and I'll puff and I'll blow your house down," and he huffed and he puffed and he blew the house down, and the little pig ran away.'

'He ate the little pig,' said William.

'No, no,' said Granny. 'The little pig ran away.'

'He ate the little pig. He ate her in a sandwich.'

'All right, he ate the little pig in a sandwich. So the second little pig –'

'You didn't tell about the tricycle.'

'What about the tricycle?'

'The wolf got on his tricycle and went to the bread shop to buy some bread. To make the sandwich,' William explained, patiently.

'Oh, well, the wolf got on his tricycle and went to the bread shop to buy some bread. And he went to the grocer's to buy some butter.' This innovation did not go down well.

'He already had some butter in the cupboard,' said William.

Learning about William

1 What do the following phrases tell us about William?

- Mummy's going to have a baby... The lady down the road had a baby. It looks like a pig.
- You make bacon out of dead pigs.
- I don't mind if it has cold feet.
- C–A–T, wheelbarrow.

- And he went to the grocer to buy some butter... He already had some butter in the cupboard.

2 What changes does William make to Granny's story?

3 What do you think will happen next in William's version?

Part 2

'So then the second little pig went for a walk and met a man with a load of wood, and the little pig said to the man, "May I have some of that wood to build a house?" and the man said, "Yes."'

'He didn't say please.'

'"Please may I have some of that wood to build a house?"'

'It was sticks.'

'Sticks are wood.'

William took out his book and turned the pages. 'That's right,' he said.

'Why don't you tell the story?' said Granny.

'I can't remember it,' said William.

'You could read it out of your book.'

'I've lost it,' said William, clutching his pullover.

'Look, do you know who this is?' He pulled a green angora scarf from under the sofa.

'No, who is it?' said Granny, glad of the diversion.

'This is Doctor Snake.' He made the scarf wriggle across the carpet.

'Why is he a doctor?'

'Because he is all furry,' said William. He wrapped the doctor round his neck and sat sucking the loose end. 'Go on about the wolf.'

'So the little pig built a house of sticks and along came the wolf – on his tricycle?'

'He came by bus. He didn't have any money for a ticket so he ate up the conductor.'

'That wasn't very nice of him,' said Granny.

'No,' said William. 'It wasn't very nice.'

'And the wolf said, "Little pig, little pig, let me come in," and the little pig said, "No," and the wolf said, "Then I'll huff and I'll puff and I'll blow your house down," so he huffed and he puffed and he blew the house down.'

'And then what did he do?' Granny asked, cautiously.

William was silent.

'Did he eat the second little pig?'

'Yes.'

'How did he eat this little pig?' said Granny, prepared for more pig sandwiches or possibly pig on toast.

'With his mouth,' said William.

'Now the third little pig went for a walk and met a man with a load of bricks. And the little pig said, "Please may I have some of those bricks to build a house?" and the man said, "Yes." So the little pig took the bricks and built a house.'

'He built it on the bomb-site.'

'Next door to the wolf?' said Granny. 'That was very silly of him.'

'There wasn't anywhere else,' said William. 'All the roads were full up.'

'The wolf didn't have to come by bus or tricycle this time, then, did he?' said Granny, grown cunning.

'Yes.' William took out the book and peered in, secretively. 'He was playing in the cemetery. He had to get another bus.'

'And did he eat the conductor this time?'

'No. A nice man gave him some money, so he bought a ticket.'

'I'm glad to hear it, said Granny.

'He ate the nice man,' said William.

William's changes

1 What further changes has William made to the story?
2 How is Granny reacting to William's behaviour? Why does she do this?
3 How do you think William's story will end?

Part 3

'So the wolf got off the bus and went up to the little pig's house, and he said, "Little pig, little pig, let me come in," and the little pig said, "No," and he huffed and he puffed and he huffed and he puffed but he couldn't blow the house down because it was made of bricks.'

'He couldn't blow it down' said William, 'because it was stuck to the ground.'

'Well, anyway, the wolf got very cross then, and he climbed on the roof and shouted down the chimney, "I'm coming to get you!" but the little pig just laughed and put a big saucepan of water on the fire.'

'He put it on the gas stove.'

'He put it on the fire,' said Granny, speaking very rapidly, 'and the wolf fell down the chimney and into the pan of water and was boiled and the little pig ate him for supper.'

William threw himself full length on the carpet and screamed.

'He didn't! He didn't! He didn't! He didn't eat the wolf.'

Granny picked him up, all stiff and kicking, and sat him on her lap.

'Did I get it wrong again, love? Don't cry. Tell me what really happened.'

William wept, and wiped his nose on Doctor Snake.

'The little pig put the saucepan on the gas stove and the wolf got down the chimney and put the little pig in the saucepan and boiled him. He had him for tea, with chips,' said William.

'Oh,' said Granny. 'I've got it all wrong, haven't I? Can I see the book, then I shall know, next time.'

William took the book from under his pullover. Granny opened it and read, First Aid for Beginners: a Practical Handbook.

'I see,' said Granny. 'I don't think I can read this. I left my glasses at home. You tell Gran how it ends.'

William turned to the last page which showed a prostrate man with his leg in a splint; compound fracture of the femur.

'Then the wolf washed up and got on his tricycle and went to see his Granny, and his Granny opened the door and said, "Hello, William."'

'I thought it was the wolf.'

'It was. It was the wolf. His name was William Wolf,' said William.

'What a nice story,' said Granny. 'You tell it much better than I do.'

'I can see up your nose,' said William. 'It's all whiskery.'

Jan Mark

Hot-seating Granny

Your teacher is going to take the role of Granny. In a pair you need to write a set of questions to find out:

- what Granny thinks of William's behaviour
- why she thinks he does some of the odd things he does
- what advice she would offer Mum

Think up your own wording for these questions. Try to avoid any questions that can be answered by just 'yes' or 'no'.

A Lot of Huff and Puff

In the following story, the wolf has been chasing a young girl, Polly, for weeks. His aim is to eat her. So far Polly has been too bright for him. That is until he gets hold of a copy of the *The Three Little Pigs* story and takes some advice from it.

At this point, he has just arrived at Polly's house and is preparing to 'blow the house down'. Polly looks on, somewhat concerned.

Clever Polly and the Stupid Wolf

The wolf doubled himself up, filled himself out and then blew with all his might. The blades of grass and the rose bushes and the clean washing waved madly in the wind, but the house never stirred at all.

'No,' said Polly, very much relieved. 'You aren't blowing down this house. It really is brick and I don't see why you should expect to be able to blow down a brick house. Even the wolf in the three little pigs' story couldn't do that. He had to climb down the chimney.'

'I thought if I practised long enough I might be able to,' the wolf said. 'After all, that incident with the pigs was a long time ago. We've probably learnt a lot about blowing since then. The wonders of Science, you know, and that sort of thing. Besides I had a book.'

From the grass beside him he picked up a small paper-covered volume and showed it to Polly. It was called *How to Become an Athlete*.

'An Ath what?' Polly asked, leaning even further out of the window.

'Good at games, that means,' the wolf explained. 'Wait a minute, there's a bit here...' He shuffled through the pages. 'Ah, yes, here we are. "Deep breathing. By constant practice of the following exercises, considerable respiratory power may be attained".'

'What sort of power?'

'You can blow very hard. I've been doing the exercises for nearly a week and I can blow much harder than before.'

'But not hard enough to blow this house down,' Polly said.

'Don't you think with some more practice–?' the wolf said hopefully.

'No,' said Polly 'I don't.'

The wolf looked crestfallen for a moment, but then he cheered up again.

'Never mind,' he said gaily. 'If I can't blow it down with my breathing exercises I'll blow it down another way.'

'How?' asked Polly...

...'I've got a thing here – it works by gunpowder, so it's awfully powerful. It'll blow the house down as soon as look at you.'

From the suitcase he produced something the size and shape of a small vegetable marrow, in a paper bag slightly too small for it.

'What is it?' Polly asked, very much interested.

'A bomb,' the wolf said, casually. 'Just a small one, but it's supposed to be able to blow up a small village or a large factory, so I should think it would about finish your little house, wouldn't you?'

...'Now,' he said, smelling it doubtfully all round. 'Somewhere, there must be something you have to do to get it to go off. The man in the shop did show me but I can't quite remember. A pin you pull out, I think or push in, or something like that.'...

...'There's a bit sticking out here. Supposing I push it in?'

Polly summoned all her courage.

'All right,' she said, as calmly as she could. 'But you know the danger?'

'What?'

'If it makes the bomb go off at once–'

'It will blow your house up,' interrupted the wolf triumphantly.

'Yes, but it will blow us up too.'

'Us?'

'Me and you. There won't be much of me left for you to eat and there won't be any of you left to be interested in eating me.'

The wolf considered this.

'You mean I might be killed?'

'If that bomb goes off while you're holding it in your hand I shouldn't think there's the slightest chance of you living any longer than me.'

'Oh,' said the wolf. He held out the bomb to Polly. 'Here,' he said generously, 'you have it, I'll give it to you as a present. I haven't got the brains for this sort of thing.'…

…'Polly,' he called out. 'Polly! When were your chimneys last swept?'

Polly couldn't help laughing, but she answered politely, 'About six months ago I think, Wolf. Why do you want to know?'

'Oh no particular reason,' said the wolf. 'I'm just interested in chimneys, that's all.'

'You must come and see ours sometime,' Polly said kindly. 'I'm afraid they're rather narrow and some of them are very twisty. And of course, none of them are quite clean. Still you could come and look from the outside. Only you'll be careful of the pot of boiling water, won't you? We always keep a pot of boiling water underneath the only big chimney, just in case anything we don't want comes down it.'

'Thank you, Polly,' said the wolf rather coldly. 'Most interesting. Another day, perhaps. Just at the moment I am rather busy.'

Catherine Storr

Talking it through

1 As a class, share your ideas about how this Three Little Pigs story has been changed.

2 Catherine Storr wrote this story for her daughter who was frightened of wolves. Look at the changes she has made; how would they reassure her daughter?

Writing a response

Look back over the two retellings and then choose to write one of these.

1 In a pair, role play and then write the conversation Granny has with William's mum about what has happened while Mum was at the clinic. Include advice on what Granny thinks is wrong and what Mum might do. Use the hot-seating activity on page 23 to help you.

2 In a group of three or four write an advice leaflet for the Wolf on how to get into Polly's house. Explain the problem of some of his ideas from the story and suggest possible methods of getting past Polly.

Taking it further

In pairs, using Catherine Storr's idea, take a famous villain from a fairy tale and place them in a modern setting. Then show how they are outwitted by the main character(s).

You could choose one of the following:

- The wicked witch in *Hansel and Gretel*
- The evil queen in *Snow White*
- The giant in *Jack and the Beanstalk*

Reread the original tale and make a note of the villain's dirty tricks. Decide how your main character will outwit them, using their intelligence and modern-day devices or ideas, e.g. converting the witch in *Hansel and Gretel* to vegetarianism.

Draft your story together and then share it with the rest of the class.

Other Worlds
Features of Science Fiction and Fantasy

This unit will look at stories which take us into another world either in the past, the future or in space. These Science Fiction and Fantasy worlds will be noticeably different from our own: animals may talk, there may be inter-galactic conflict, battles may occur involving super-human powers.

The video clip from *Elidor* shows one journey into another world. Using this clip and the extract from *Elidor* on page 28, begin your discussion about the typical ingredients of a fantasy adventure.

What are the ingredients?

Below are extracts from three well-known novels, two involving fantasy worlds and the other a science fiction adventure.

1 To consider the particular ingredients of these stories, read through the extracts with a partner and make a list of typical settings, characters, events, and places.

2 Then enter these elements on your copy of the chart on page 29. Finally, add any further ingredients you can think of including the titles of books and films that these ingredients come from.

Planet of the Warlord

It was a search that had begun for Keill Randor on the terrible day when he returned to his planet, Moros, and found a dead world, enveloped in a strange radiation that had wiped out all life. Keill himself had come close enough to be touched by the edge of the radiation, and afterwards found that the radiation had entered his bones, and was slowly killing him.

In the time he had left, Keill had gone out among the Inhabited Worlds on a relentless quest for some clue to the identity of the murderer of Moros. But it had seemed hopeless. No one had any information, and his time was running out. Yet, meanwhile, others had been seeking him.

He had been gathered up by a group of mysterious brilliant scientists, whom he came to know as the Overseers. And with their amazing skills and knowledge, they had healed him – by replacing his radiated bones. They gave him a new skeletal structure, made of a unique organic alloy – with a special side-effect. The material was virtually unbreakable.

If that had astonished Keill, he was astonished even more by the story that the Overseers had told him, through their elderly leader, Talis. Keill learned that the Overseers too were seeking the murderer of Moros, and had been doing so for some time before the attack on the Legions.

Talis told him that they had become aware of an evil force at work among the Inhabited Worlds. They had been unable to learn who or what it might be, or where it was located. But its intentions were plain to the Overseers, in their wide-ranging study of galactic events.

The force, or being, was dedicated to stirring up the horror of war wherever possible among mankind's worlds. So the Overseers had given that unknown being a suitable name. They had called him... the Warlord.

The Warlord seemed to be using the old human failings – greed, fear, bigotry, power, hunger – to turn people towards war, to set race against race, planet against planet. It became clear that his ultimate aim was to spread the infection so widely that the whole galaxy would be plunged into conflict. And out of the ruins of that final holocaust, the Warlord would emerge – to rule supreme over what was left of the Inhabited Worlds.

Douglas Hill

The Hobbit

Now he shot with a great yew bow, till all his arrows but one were spent. The flames were near him. His companions were leaving him. He bent his bow for the last time.

Suddenly out of the dark something fluttered to his shoulder. He started – but it was only an old thrush. Unafraid, it perched by his ear and it brought him news. Marvelling he found he could understand its tongue, for he was of the race of Dale.

'Wait! Wait!' it said to him. 'The moon is rising. Look for the hollow of the left breast as he flies and turns above you!' And while Bard paused in wonder it told him of tidings up in the Mountain and of all that it had heard.

Then Bard drew his bow-string to his ear. The dragon was circling back, flying low, and as he came the moon rose above the eastern shore and silvered his great wings.

'Arrow!' said the bowman. 'Black arrow! I have saved you to the last. You have never failed me and always I have recovered you. I had you from my father and he from of old. If ever you came from the forges of the true king under the Mountain, go now and speed well!'

The dragon swooped once more lower than ever, and as he turned and dived down his belly glittered white with sparkling fires of gems in the moon – but not in one place. The great bow twanged. The black arrow sped straight from the string, straight for the hollow by the left breast where the foreleg was flung wide. In it smote and vanished, barb, shaft, and feather, so fierce was its flight. With a shriek that deafened men, felled trees, and split stone, Smaug shot spouting into the air, turned over, and crashed down from on high in ruin.

J R R Tolkien

Elidor

The footsteps reached the stairs and began
to climb.

'Who's there?'

'Do not be afraid,' said a voice.

'Who are you? What do you want?'

The footsteps were at the top of the stairs.
A shadow fell across the landing.

'No,' cried Roland. 'Don't come any
nearer!'

The fiddler stood in the doorway.

'I shall not harm you. Take the end of
my bow, and lead me...

...Help me.'

'All – all right.'

Roland put his hand forward to take the bow, but as he was about
to touch it a shock struck his finger tips, driving light through his
forehead between the eyes. It was as though a shutter had been lifted
in his mind, and in the moment before it dropped again he saw
something; but it went so quickly that all he could hold was the shape
of its emptiness.

'What did you see?'

'See? I didn't – see. I – through my fingers – See? Towers – like flame.
A candle in darkness. A black wind.'...

...'I can't stay,' said Roland. But the old
man put the fiddle to his shoulder. 'I'm
looking for my sister, and my two brothers –'
The old man began to play. '– and I must
find them before dark –' It was a wild dance.
' – and we've a train to catch. What's that
noise? – Please! – Stop! – It's hurting! –
Please! – '

The air took up the fiddle's note. It was
the sound Roland had heard upstairs, but
now it was louder, building waves that jarred
until he felt that he was threaded on the
sound.

' – Please! – '

'Now! Open the door!'

'I can't! It's locked!'

'Open it! There is little time!'

'But – !'

'Now!'

Roland stumbled to the door, grasped the iron handle and pulled with all his weight. The door opened, and he ran out onto the cobbles of the street, head down, driven by the noise.

But he never reached the far pavement, for the cobbles were moving under him. He turned. The outline of the church rippled in the air, and vanished. He was standing among boulders on a seashore, and the music died into the crash of breakers, and the long fall of surf.

Alan Garner

Ingredients in Science Fiction and Fantasy

Typical Settings

Alien planets

Typical Characters

The dwarf
Helper with unusual powers

Typical Events

Inter-galactic conflict
Entry to another world

Typical Places

Starship

Titles

The Hobbit
Planet of the Warlord
Elidor

Pooling ideas

When you have completed the chart with your partner, pool ideas as a class to build up your table of ingredients further.

Look back at the extracts to help you. You might also consider books from your own reading, such as *The Hitchhiker's Guide to the Galaxy*, *Red Dwarf*, *The Deptford Mice*, the *Narnia* series, and *The Earthsea Trilogy*.

Spotting the Pattern

Steps in a hero's journey

Science Fiction and Fantasy tales often centre around a hero/heroine who has to make a special journey to find something. This is called a 'quest' plot. A **plot** is the series of events in a story.

This chart shows a pattern that is typical of a 'quest' plot. Christopher Vogler came up with this, after looking at stories from many cultures. He works in the Disney Animation Department of Hollywood. This plot pattern has been important in the planning and making of *The Lion King*, *Aladdin*, and *Beauty and The Beast*. As you can see, *Star Wars* and *Romancing the Stone* follow the same pattern.

1 In a group of four or five, read through the 12 stages in the chart Can you think of events from science fiction or fantasy stories that fit all or part of the pattern?

2 Choose one story, add the title and particular events for each stage in the far right-hand columm. The first few stages of *The Hobbit* have been put in to give you the idea.
You will be given your own copy of the chart to fill in.
You may want to consider the titles suggested at the bottom of page 29 as well as films like *Back to the Future*, *Flash Gordon*, *Who Killed Roger Rabbit?*, *Robin Hood*, *Prince of Thieves*, and *Batman*.

The 12 Steps of the Hero's Journey

KRIEG · Star Wars

#	Step		Star Wars
1	ORDINARY WORLD	Hero/heroine in original surroundings	Restless teenager Luke Skywalker is bored with life on the remote farm where he lives with his uncle and aunt. His parents are presumed dead and he feels incomplete.
2	CALL TO ADVENTURE	Unsatisfied – hears challenge	Luke accidentally finds the beautfiul Princess Leia's deperate plea for help addressed to Obi-Wan Kenobi, and stored in the droid R2D2.
3	REFUSAL OF THE CALL	First reaction is to back away	Luke seeks out Obi-Wan Kenobi but doesn't dare take up the challenge, saying that his uncle and aunt need him.
4	MEETING THE MENTOR	Figure arrives to help encourage hero/heroine	Luke finally puts himself in the hands of Obi-Wan and begins to learn about the Force.
5	CROSSING THE FIRST THRESHOLD	Enters into new world/challenge	Luke takes up the challenge when Imperial troops barbecue his uncle and aunt.
6	TESTS, ALLIES, ENEMIES	Adventures to test heroism and build character	Luke and Obi-Wan head for a spaceport bar, meet up with Han Solo and the Wookie and make a bitter enemy of Jabba the Hut.
7	APPROACH TO THE INMOST CAVE	Arrive at what he/she sought after	Luke and company have a series of adventures that culminate in an attempt to break the Princess out of the Deathstar.
8	SUPREME ORDEAL	Struggle for power	The ordeal is made up of a series of adventures in the Deathstar, including a near-death experience in garbage compactor.
9	REWARD (SEIZING THE SWORD)	Gains what he/she wants	Luke and company escape with the Princess and the information needed to destroy the Deathstar, but not without the sacrifice of Obi-Wan.
10	ROAD BACK	Enemies threaten return journey	The worst is not yet over: the Deathstar, moving within range of the rebel base, still has to be destroyed.
11	RESURRECTION	Conflict where hero/heroine learns about self	Luke trusts the Force and destroys the Deathstar by sacrificing an old part of his personality, his dependence on machines.
12	RETURN WITH ELIXIR	Return with greater knowledge	Luke and friends are decorated as heroes in front of a large crowd. Luke's internal elixir is his new self-knowledge and control of the Force.

Romancing the Stone

The Hobbit

Title

Romantic novelist, Joan Wilder, lives in a cluttered New York appartment and there is no partner in her life. She dreams of finding a true love and adventure.	Bilbo Baggins lives at Bag End.
Joan receives a phone call from her sister, who has been kidnapped by thugs in Columbia.	Gandalf arrives at Bag End looking for a hero.
Joan is a willing hero, but the refusal is acknowledged in a scene with her tough, cynical agent who tells her: 'You're not cut out for this.'	Bilbo tells Gandalf he is not interested.
Joan's agent is a negative influence and attempts to prevent her from answering the call.	Dwarves arrive with tales to persuade Bilbo.
Joan arrives in Columbia and is immediately misdirected onto a bus that is going nowhere.	Bilbo gets to Green Dragon at 11.00 in time to leave with the dwarves.
Joan is followed by a sinister man, the bus crashes, she is 'rescued' by the archetypal Shapeshifter, Jack, more a mercenary than an ally.	
On the run from the baddies, Joan and Jack seek out the hiding place of El Corazon, a giant emerald, using the map the kidnappers are after.	
Joan and Jack quickly locate the emerald in a real inmost cave, but that is too easy and their car plunges over a waterfall. Joan disappears for several seconds, finally struggling to a rock on the opposite side from Jack.	
The obvious reward is possession of the gem, but Joan has also found romance and new self-knowledge.	
The river separates them and the two have to make their own way out of the jungle. Joan has to trust that Jack, who has the gem, will keep his promise.	
Joan and Jack unite to rescue her sister, but Jack immediately pursues his own interest, the money. She has to give up her hopes of love, but is changed by her adventures.	
A changed Joan, more 'together' and a better writer, has surrendered her old fantasies about men, when Jack appears with the sailing boat he always dreamed of, to whisk her away.	

Adventure on Venda

Background on Venda

Now you have the opportunity to use the ideas raised in this unit in your own fantasy adventure.

On the planet Venda, the warlord Orxis has developed Ossidin, a lethal and long-lasting source of radiation. He intends to use this to destroy any planets that defy his leadership and is preparing his weapon carriers for launch into space to begin his attack.

You have been sent from the planet Marron to destroy the Ossidin control panel in Orxis' Space Centre and exterminate Orxis. However, you also know that he is defended by the forces of The Deathwing: Demos, and Santis.

Your allies in the Space Centre are:

Pathfinder

A metallic eagle with eyes that can see long distances and which has the power of speech. He has great stamina and can chart a path through enemy territory while scouting for possible danger. Frightened of fire.

Asgard

A slight woman who, while she appears human has great powers of healing and hunting. She can see in the dark, but is vulnerable in combat and in the cold.

Draxis

A fearless fighter with great leadership qualities. He can raise a tired team to battle, is a master at strategy. He carries an electron sword and wears a rope girdle.

Using the warm-air ducts you successfully enter the Space Centre and destroy the control panel. Orxis, recognizing the danger has fled, but not before setting Demos and Santis the task of destroying you. You must get out of the centre alive, and destroy your enemies so you can pursue Orxis who is on the way to your ship.

Your enemies in the Space Centre are:

Demos

A mutant from the Planet Cerus. He has elongated arms and legs of tremendous power that make him a formidable wrestler and very agile. He has a tough leathery outer skin that forms a protective coat except for a patch behind one knee. His grip will strangle and mutilate in seconds.

Santis

A thin, sinewy android with acrobatic balance and very quick reflexes. Protected by an armoured body suit, she has a bracelet that emits a lethal electric beam. This can counteract Draxis' electron sword.

This map of Venda should give you an idea of the terrain that you will have to cross.

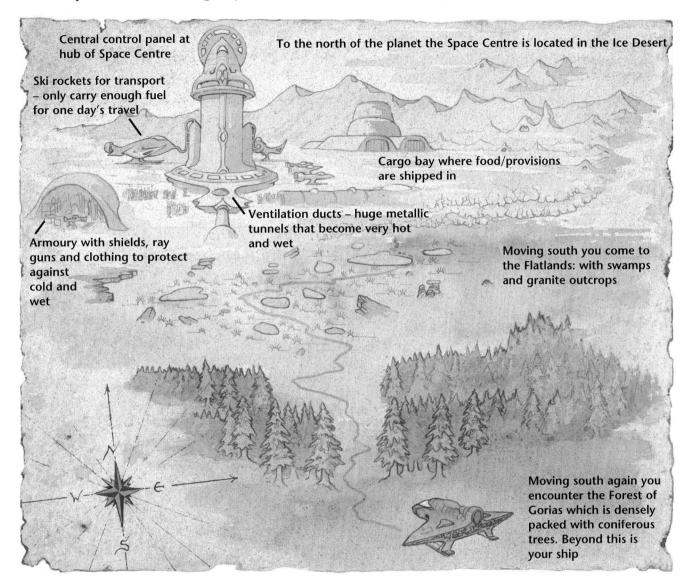

Central control panel at hub of Space Centre

Ski rockets for transport – only carry enough fuel for one day's travel

Armoury with shields, ray guns and clothing to protect against cold and wet

Ventilation ducts – huge metallic tunnels that become very hot and wet

To the north of the planet the Space Centre is located in the Ice Desert

Cargo bay where food/provisions are shipped in

Moving south you come to the Flatlands: with swamps and granite outcrops

Moving south again you encounter the Forest of Gorias which is densely packed with coniferous trees. Beyond this is your ship

Taking your instructions

Read all the background information, and then, very carefully follow these instructions.

1 Make sure you understand all the details about both your enemies and your allies.

2 Study the map of the Space Centre and the terrain around it carefully.

3 You first task is to escape safely from the Centre, but you will need the following:
- food/provisions for the journey home
- additional weaponry
- transport if possible (but this is not essential)

4 Decide on your route.

5 Decide how to carry the weapons and food you obtain.

Writing Chapter 1

Write the story of how you and your companions escape. If you look back at the chart on pages 30–31 – 'The 12 Steps of the Hero's Journey' – you are dealing with Stages 8 and 9. You could include the kind of action from your chart on page 29 that has happened in other stories/films.

Chapter 2

Having escaped from the Space Centre you are now stranded in the Ice Desert. The terrain is treacherous with narrow rocky paths covered in ice. You have found shelter in a small ice cave on a narrow ledge. Pathfinder has flown out to scout the territory, while you begin to light a fire.

Suddenly, a vicious flapping of wings and high pitched screeching makes you realize that you are the prey of two Warlocks.

Warlocks

These are huge birds with scaly bodies, vast leathery wings, and talons like razor blades. They attack prey with their vicious beaks but are frightened of fire.

Taking more instructions

1 Decide how your party can defend themselves.
2 Decide whether anyone gets injured in the attack.
3 If so, how do you help the injured?
4 Now tell the story of the battle with the Warlocks in Chapter 2.

To venture back on the main path would be madness, but you need to move on.

Chapter 3

You are now clear of the desert and have entered the marshy Flatlands. Then Pathfinder flies down with a worried expression on his face: the land ahead has a patch on it that appears to be moving. He believes he has spotted ten Spike worms heading in this direction. They have picked up your party's scent.

Spike worms

These are three metres in length and move very rapidly. They have a tough green skin with a collar of long needle-sharp spines. The tips are covered with venom, and unless treated immediately one jab would be fatal. The worms cannot see well yet have acute hearing. Given their wet skins they are vulnerable to electricity.

Taking further instructions

1 Decide what preparations you make for defending your group.
2 What happens when the Spike worms arrive?
3 Is anyone hurt and if so how do you deal with it?

Writing Chapter 3

Tell the story of what happens when the Spike worms attack. Chapter 3 matches Stage 10 in the 'The 12 Steps of the Hero's Journey' chart on pages 30–31. So, once again, consider what happens in other stories/films at this stage and you can add these events to your own ideas.

Chapter 4

You are tired and battle-worn from the meeting with the Spike worms and have reached the Forest of Gorias. This is close to your ship, but the forest is dense and progress will be slow. In addition, you know that Orxis is ahead, and you must capture him before he reaches your base.

As you make camp, Asgard becomes worried because she senses Orxis close by. Suddenly, the air is filled with a white vapour and you begin to lose consciousness. As you sink to the floor you hear Asgard screeching at you and feel her trying to pull you up.

Final instructions

1 When you wake up, what has Orxis done?
2 How can your party counter this and attack him?
3 How will you reach your ship?
4 As you radio Marron, what can you tell them about the number of survivors and the success of the mission?

Taking it further

Write the last part of this story from the point of view of both Asgard and yourself, explaining the two stages of escape:

■ from Orxis in the wood
■ from the planet of Venda

Try to include ideas from Stages 11 and 12 of the 'The 12 Steps of a Hero's Journey' chart in your own narrative.

Language Study
Proper Nouns

Labelling particular people, places, and things

Look back at the opening of 'Adventure on Venda' on page 32. The opening sentence reads:

> 'On the planet *Venda*, the warlord *Orxis* has developed *Ossidin*, a lethal and long-lasting source of radiation.'

The three highlighted words are all names. Venda is the name of a particular planet, Orxis the name of a particular person, Ossidin the name of a particular weapon.

This kind of word – which labels a particular person, place or thing – is called a **proper noun**. Proper nouns always begin with a capital letter.

The emerald – El Corazon

Joan and Jack

Deathstar

Finding proper nouns

Look back at 'The 12 Steps in the Hero's Journey' on pages 30–31 and find:

- 10 examples of proper nouns which name particular people (robots and monsters can count as people!)
- 4 examples of proper nouns which label particular places
- 2 examples of proper nouns which label particular things

Sentences and their Punctuation

Full stops, question marks, and exclamation marks

Look at each of these sentences from *Clever Polly and the Stupid Wolf* on pages 24–25.

It will blow your house up.

Polly!

What is it?

Here, you have it.

Each sentence ends in a different punctuation mark.

■ The first sentence is a **statement** and ends in a **full stop**.

■ The second is a **question** and ends in a **question mark**.

■ The third is an **exclamation** and ends in an **exclamation mark**.

■ The fourth is a **command** and ends in a **full stop** (although sometimes a command can end in an *exclamation mark*).

Statements

Most of the sentences you read are likely to be statements. Polly's first speech in *Clever Polly and the Stupid Wolf* is made up of a series of statements, one after the other:

> 'No,' said Polly, very much relieved. 'You aren't blowing down this house. It really is brick…'

It is very common for stories to begin and end with statements.

Two obvious examples are:

> Once upon a time, there was a Princess.
>   and
> And they lived happily ever after.

Look back at *The Great Rain, How the Elephant Became* and *How Crab Got its Back* on pages 10–13 and 16–17.

1 Write down the statement sentences which open and conclude each story.

2 Read through one of these stories again and pick out 8 to 10 statement sentences which can be put together to summarize the main events of the story. Compare your choice with someone else's. Did you find it difficult having to stick to statements? Pick out any questions, exclamations or commands which might have been more useful.

Questions

Asking the reader

Questions are not common in stories (except in dialogue, as you will see). Some retellings of myths, legends, and folk-tales do include them, however, and there are two examples in *How the Elephant Became*:

> But what did become of him in the end? Where is he now?

In these examples, the story-teller is involving their reader or listener. The questions draw the reader into the story and invite them to predict the way it might turn out.

Questions in dialogue

When we include dialogue in stories, there are likely to be a large number of questions, because that is the way normal speech works.

William's Version on pages 18–23 contains a lot of dialogue and is full of questions. These are mainly asked by Granny, but there are a few points at which William asks a question.

For example, when Granny challenges William to read out of his book, he changes the subject by reaching for his scarf and asking:

> 'Look, do you know who this is?'

In pairs, find three other questions that William asks Granny and write them down.

What do they tell us about what's going on in William's head while Granny is trying to tell the story?

Exclamations and Commands

Different uses

To exclaim means to 'cry out', for example in surprise or amusement. The most common uses of exclamation marks are to show that:

A a command has been given, e.g. 'Come here!'
B something has been said rather sharply, e.g. 'No!'
C something is urgent, e.g. 'Quick!'

They can also be used when something is said:

D forcefully, e.g. 'You will go!'
E with surprise, e.g. 'It can't be!'
F decisively, e.g. 'I've got it!'
G with some powerful emotion, such as anger, e.g. 'I hate you!
H or amusement, e.g. 'He's fallen in!'
I a loud noise is made, e.g. 'Quack!' or 'Cuckoo!'

The examples that follow are all taken from the dialogue in *The Great Rain*.

In pairs, find each one in the story. Then choose a reason from the list opposite to show why the exclamation mark was used, e.g. 1 = B

1 'Thunderbird!' she called.
2 '...I'm angry!'
3 '...Kaaa!'
4 'Yes! That's it!'
5 'Listen to me, people!'
6 'That will be very wet indeed, old woman!'
7 'The lightning is dancing with us!'
8 'You deserve to drown, all of you!'

Commas

Read each of these sentences or phrases, all of which are from extracts used in the Narrative module.

A Yolanda was beautiful, proud, haughty and lazy.

B 'I can't remember it,' said William.

C As the boat heaved up and down and whirled round in circles, as the lightning flashed and the thunder roared, the two of them fought in the tiny boat.

D It came in so far, in fact, that the old man…

E …when he returned to his planet, Moros, and found a dead world…

F '…Thank you, Polly…'

Each of those examples shows a different use of one of the most important punctuation marks: the **comma**. The comma can help to break up sentences and make them easier to read.

The most important uses

The most common and important uses of the comma are these.

1 In lists

Sentence **A** shows how commas are used to separate words in lists:

e.g. …beautiful, proud, haughty…

Find examples in the extracts from *The Hobbit* and *Planet of the Warlord* on pages 26–27 where commas are used in lists of nouns.

2 In dialogue

There will always be a punctuation mark at the end of someone's speech in a piece of dialogue. If the sentence has not ended (for example, because the speech will be followed by 'said William'), you use a comma:

e.g. 'I can't remember it,' said William.

(If William had been asking a question, or exclaiming, you would use a question mark or exclamation mark instead. For more on the punctuation of dialogue see page 152.)

Look for other examples in *William's Version* on pages 18–23 where commas are used at the end of speeches in dialogue.

3 To make sentences clearer

The comma can make a longer sentence easier to read, by showing the reader how it can be divided up:

e.g. …as the lightning flashed and the thunder roared, the two of them fought in the tiny boat.

Reread the final paragraph of *The Hobbit* extract on page 27 and find examples of the comma used in this way.

Read this extract carefully and then look at the uses of the commas. In pairs, decide whether each comma has been used for reason 1, 2, or 3.

As Charlie emptied the shopping basket, his mother stood by in some surprise. She could see why he might want the apples, honey, Rice Krispies, *The Beano* and chewing gum. But the rest of the items were a complete mystery, even allowing for the fact that he was not an experienced shopper.

Batteries, plasters, a pack of toilet rolls…

'It's for Scout camp next week,' he explained, but not before he gave her one final, withering look.

Deciding on the Right Punctuation

On page 16 of the Narrative module, you read *How the Elephant Became.* Here is another of Ted Hughes' animal creation myths: *Why the Owl Behaves as He Does.* You will notice that most of the punctuation marks have been left out.

Making decisions

In pairs, try to insert punctuation which will help the story to make sense. In Part A, the full stops and capital letters have been left in but you still have to decide where to add commas which will make the sentences easier to understand.

The task is harder in Part B, where all the punctuation is missing apart from speech marks. Follow these steps.

1 Read the passage carefully, trying to get as much meaning out of it as you can.

2 Divide it up into sentences which make sense and tell the story clearly.

3 Look at each sentence and put the correct punctuation mark at the end, according to whether the sentence is a statement, question, exclamation, or command.

4 Finally, think where the commas might make the sentences clearer.

Before you start, reread *How the Elephant Became* in order to remind yourself of how Hughes tells a story.

You will be given your own copy of the story to mark the punctuation on.

Why the Owl Behaves As He Does

Part A

Owl realizing he is the only bird who can see at night decides to fool the other birds. He tells them there is another land with no cats or farmers with guns so they will be safe. They agree to follow him there so he leads them in the dark of a rabbit hole and goes round and round until dusk. As they come up he says day is breaking. They notice that it is getting darker and then he tells them that in this land day is dark and night is so dark one glimpse of it and birds die. As the birds pick for food in the dark he swoops down and kills the smaller ones. As dark starts to fade he tells them to close their eyes for safety and he sleeps on as they sit terrified. Life is so grim that eventually one bird keeps its eyes open and sees day. Owl is found out.

Part B

'He tricked us' they cried 'and there he goes there goes the trickster' in a shouting mob all the birds flocked after Owl all the way back to his tree they beat him with their wings and pulled out his feathers he buried himself deep in his hollow tree the birds flew up to the tree top and sang on and on and so it is still every morning the birds sing and the owl flies back to his dark hole when birds see him they mob him remembering his trick he dare come out only at night to scrape a bare living on rats and mice and beetles.

Ted Hughes

Poem as Story
Cautionary Tales

A twist in the tail

The story poems in this unit combine the funny and the serious. Often written with a moral, the rhyme allows for laughter, and a twist in the tail.

You will probably recognize the story on page 43. With Roald Dahl's treatment, there's an unexpected twist. To start with, just read it through on your own.

Poetry in performance

One of the best ways to enjoy most cautionary tales, and particularly this one, is as a group performance with different individuals taking the parts of different characters.

In groups of four, prepare a rehearsed reading of the tale. The aim is to bring your individual character to life and make your audience laugh at the right times! Begin by making notes around your part of the poem to prompt you when you are reading. (Your teacher will give you a copy.)

As a group you will need to consider:
- who will read which part
- what each character is like, using clues from the text
- tone of voice for different lines
- which words to emphasize
- do you want to echo or repeat any lines/words/phrases as you would in a 'round' in music?
- the pace – where will you go fast/slow?
- the volume – which parts will be loud/ soft?
- sound effects, e.g. telephone ringing
- where you will place readers during the performance
- how you will perform, i.e. in front of the class or on to a tape recorder?

The notes below may give you ideas on how the script can be marked. You can make up your own signs and markings.

For another retelling of a fairy tale see pages 24–25 in the Narrative module.

As soon as Wolf began to feel — Wolf could rub tummy
That he would like a decent meal, — Wolf grins
He went and knocked on Grandma's door. — Very polite and gentle
When Grandma opened it, she saw
The sharp white teeth, the horrid grin, — Rising panic – up pace and volume
And Wolfie said, 'May I come in?' —
Poor Grandmamma was terrified, — (Pause)
'He's going to eat me up!' she cried. — Fast and high in pitch
And she was absolutely right. — Stress 'absolutely'
He ate her up in one big bite. — Slow down for 'one big bite'
But Grandmamma was small and tough,
And Wolfie wailed, 'That's not enough!' — Long and miserable

▢ Narrator
▢ Grandma
▢ Wolf

Little Red Riding Hood and The Wolf

As soon as Wolf began to feel
That he would like a decent meal,
He went and knocked on Grandma's door.
When Grandma opened it, she saw
The sharp white teeth, the horrid grin,
And Wolfie said, 'May I come in?'
Poor Grandmamma was terrified,
'He's going to eat me up!' she cried.
And she was absolutely right.
He ate her up in one big bite.
But Grandmamma was small and tough,
And Wolfie wailed, 'That's not enough!
'I haven't yet begun to feel
'That I have had a decent meal!'
He ran around the kitchen yelping,
'I've *got* to have another helping!'
Then added with a frightful leer,
'I'm therefore going to wait right here
'Till Little Miss Riding Hood
'Comes home from walking in the wood.'
He quickly put on Grandma's clothes,
(Of course he hadn't eaten those).
He dressed himself in coat and hat.
He put on shoes and after that
He even brushed and curled his hair,
Then sat himself in Grandma's chair.
In came the little girl in red.
She stopped. She stared. And then she said,

'*What great big ears you have, Grandma.*'
'*All the better to hear you with,*' the Wolf replied.
'*What great big eyes you have, Grandma,*'
    said Little Red Riding Hood.
'*All the better to see you with,*' the Wolf replied.

He sat there watching her and smiled.
He thought, I'm going to eat this child.
Compared with her old Grandmamma
She's going to taste like caviare.

Then Little Red Riding Hood said, 'But Grandma,
    what a lovely great big furry coat you have on.'
'That's wrong!' cried Wolf. 'Have you forgot
'To tell me what BIG TEETH I've got?
'Ah well, no matter what you say,
'I'm going to eat you anyway.'
The small girl smiles. One eyelid flickers.
She whips a pistol from her knickers.
She aims it at the creature's head
And bang bang bang, she shoots him dead.
A few weeks later, in the wood,
I came across Miss Riding Hood.
But what a change! No cloak of red,
No silly hood upon her head.
She said, 'Hello, and do please note
'My lovely furry WOLFSKIN COAT.'

Roald Dahl

Reading the Whole Story

Piecing the tale together

1 Now have a go at reconstructing and rewriting another famous cautionary tale with a more serious ending. The section of the poem on this page is printed correctly, so use this and the pictures to get into the story.

Matilda
Who Told Lies, and Was Burnt To Death

Matilda told such Dreadful Lies,
It made one Gasp and Stretch one's Eyes;
Her Aunt, who from her Earliest Youth,
Had kept a Strict Regard for Truth,
Attempted to Believe Matilda:
The effort very nearly killed her,
And would have done so, had not She
Discovered this Infirmity.
For once, towards the Close of Day,
Matilda, growing tired of play,
And finding she was left alone...
Went tiptoe
           to
                the Telephone
And summoned the Immediate Aid
Of London's Noble Fire Brigade.
Within an hour the Gallant Band
Were pouring in on every hand,
From Putney, Hackney Downs and Bow,
With Courage High and Hearts a-glow
They galloped, roaring through the Town.
'Matilda's House is Burning Down!'

2 In the next section of the poem, the lines have been printed in the wrong order. Use the following clues to put the lines in the right order:

- the pictures
- story so far
- the title
- the rhyme pattern of the first section

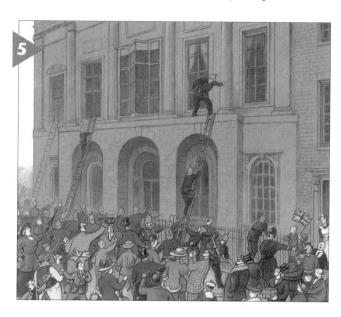

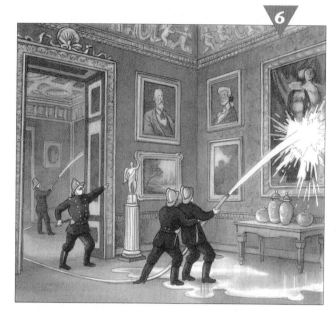

Of windows on the Ball Room Floor;
The Second Mrs Tanqueray.
And took Peculiar Pains to Souse
To get the Men to go away!
She had refused to take her Niece
The pictures up and down the House,
It happened that a few Weeks later
They ran their ladders through a score
Her Aunt was off to the Theatre
Inspired by British Cheers and Loud
A Deprivation Just and Wise
Proceeding from the Frenzied Crowd,
Until Matilda's Aunt succeeded
To Punish her for Telling Lies.
And even then she had to pay
To see that Interesting Play
In showing them they were not needed
To hear this Entertaining Piece:

3 In the final section, on page 47, you will need to supply some of the missing lines to finish the story. You have been given seven full lines and the end rhyme of each line.

In pairs, use the pictures, punctuation, and story so far to finish it off. To start yourself off, try retelling this part of the story in your own words using just the pictures and then try to make your ideas fit the empty spaces.

That Night a Fire did break out –
_____ shout!
You should have heard her Scream and Bawl,
_____ call
_____ Street –
(The rapidly increasing Heat
Encouraging her to obtain
Their confidence) but all in vain!
_____ 'Fire!'
They only answered 'Little Liar!'
And therefore when her Aunt returned,
_____ burned.

Hillaire Belloc

Taking it further

Compare your version with the original (you will be given a copy).
Then, using the guidelines on page 42, prepare a performed
reading like the one of Roald Dahl's *Little Red Riding Hood and the
Wolf*. After you have done your performance, watch the version on
the video. How does it compare with yours?

Drafting a Story Poem

Everyone loves a good story

Poets often make a good story the backbone of their work.

The poem below tells a story rather like a film, in a series of pictures. As you read this poem try to picture the events that are being described and the mood of the person telling the story.

The Shoes

These are the shoes
Dad walked about in
When we did jobs
In the garden,
When his shed
Was full of shavings,
When he tied
The fence up,
When my old bike
Needed mending,
When the car
Could not get started,
When he got up late
On Sunday.
These are the shoes
Dad walked about in
And I've kept them
In my room.

These are not the shoes
That Dad walked out in
When we didn't know
Where he was going.
When I tried to lift
His suitcase,
When he said goodbye
And kissed me,
When he left his door-key
On the table,
When he promised Mum
He'd send a postcard,
When I couldn't hear
His special footsteps.
These are not the shoes
That Dad walked out in,
But he'll need them
When he comes back.

John Mole

Sharing ideas

1 In rough, on a piece of paper complete the following statements...

- ■ I think this poem is about...
- ■ I think the best lines/phrases are... because
- ■ I think the person telling the story feels...
- ■ The scenes I can picture most clearly are...

2 Share your original jottings with a partner and see how closely you agree.

Drafting a poem: from a father's point of view

Poems do not just 'appear' in their finished state. They often take a number of attempts or **drafts**. To show you how this works, you have the drafts of another writer, trying to produce their own version of *The Shoes*, writing from a father's point of view. Begin by working on the writer's version below. Read through stage 1 and develop your own ideas at the end of stages 2 and 3, using the guidelines given to you.

1 Poems often start out as notes based on a single line, word or phrase that has a particular significance. For example, in this poem it is:

These are the shoes....

That word, phrase or line leads on to others that are similar. These may follow in a logical order but more likely they will tumble over each other in no particular order at all.

This is the brainstorming stage.

> These are the shoes
>   she wore through that autumn
>   that pinched on the heel
> scuffed after a fall from her bicycle
>   that taught her to tie laces
> that she rattled on the chair legs
>   splattered through November puddles

2 Some writers like to write in prose first before they shape their writing into a more rhythmic pattern. So their notes might look like this.

These are the shoes that she wore through that autumn of '88 when we learnt to ride her first bicycle; the shoes that scuffed like her kneecaps where she came off; that she rattled as she sat, bored in her highchair; that we'd gently prise off her tired feet; that splattered and slapped through autumn puddles; that would kick themselves under my arms as she rode on my shoulders. These are the shoes she toddled about in and I've kept them in my case.

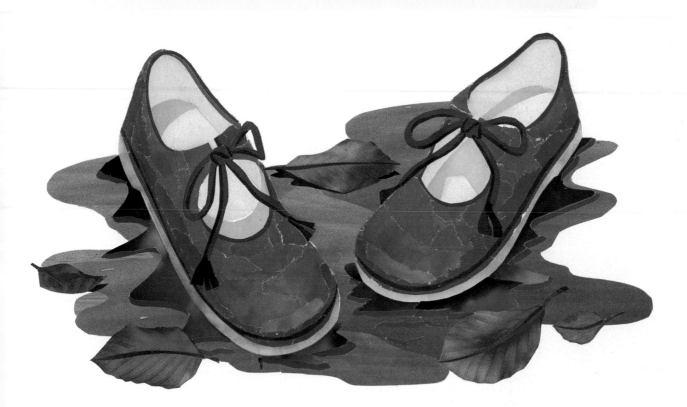

To divide this prose into lines of poetry, you have to decide where the line breaks are going to come.

Copy these notes out and try marking line breaks with a / to see what shape you think this piece could take.

3 In the next draft, as well as lines, there are extra notes and word changes. See if you can identify these.
Do you think they improve the piece? If so, how?

```
These are the shoes
She shuffled about in
When we learnt
To tie laces;
That splattered and slapped/chuckled and
Through November puddles,
Which would hang
From my shoulders
These are the shoes
That hung from my shoulders
On Sunday excursions
When her head
Was filled with questions.
When she declared
'Shoes not sooes',
These are the shoes
She strutted off in,
And I've kept them
In my case…
Just in case.


Anne Powling
```

Taking it further

1 When you read the poem again, you might want to edit the draft further. You could:
  - alter line order
  - put in different ideas
  - change words
  - add another section like John Mole's on what the shoes did not do that show regrets and sadness
  - compare your final versions with each other
2 You may like to work on a completely original version of the story poem on your own, putting in all your ideas and working through the drafting stages yourself.

Poem as Picture
Pictures in Writing

Appealing to your senses

A poem should be like taking a photograph. It should capture a place, time, and emotion so you can experience it vividly. A poet creates a word picture.

These poems all create a vivid portrait of a city. In pairs, each read aloud one poem to your partner. Then make a list of key phrases which help you to:

- see the city
- hear the city
- smell, and touch the city

Zebra

white sun
black
fire escape.

morning
grazing like a zebra
outside my window.

Judith Thurman

Song of the City

My brain is stiff with concrete
My limbs are rods of steel
My belly's stuffed with money
My soul was bought in a deal.

They poured metal through my arteries
They choked my lungs with lead
They churned my blood to plastic
They put murder in my head.

I'd a face like a map of the weather
Flesh that grew to the bone
But they tore my story out of my eyes
And turned my heart to stone.

Let me wind from my source like a river
Let me grow like wheat from the grain
Let me hold out my arms like a natural tree
Let my children love me again.

Gareth Owen

George Square

George Square
idleness
an island
children splashing
in a sea of pigeons
pigeons strutting
pigeon-toed.

And we
city dwellers
sitting
separate
close together.
City dwellers
we only know
nature captive –
zoos and gardens
Latin tagged.
We know no earth
or roots.
We see no slow
season shift
but sudden summer
blaze a concrete day
and catch us unawares.
We can find no sense
in traffic lights'
continual change of emphasis.

Nature captive:
this is a city
nature's barred.
But the flowers
bound and bedded
bloom
incurable as cancer
and as for fat old ladies'
flowery
summer dresses
my god, they really are
a riot.

Liz Lochhead

Creating an image collage

Now choose one poem from page 52 and match your key phrases and lines to appropriate pictures from newspapers and magazines. Create an image collage like this one for *George Square*. You could work on this with your partner or team up with another pair.

You can learn more about why Liz Lochhead chose these images for *George Square* from the interview with her on the video.

Writing an alphabet picture

Using your ideas and the title 'City Scene', you are going to compose a word picture using the alphabet as your structure.

Each letter of the alphabet becomes the occupation or object which starts a line. Every line should paint a picture of something that is happening in the city .

This example should get you started, but work on your own original ideas. You can write individually or work in a group and use a thesaurus to help you find suitable words.

City Scene

<u>A</u>mbulances angle through crowded city streets.
<u>B</u>uilders battle with waste ground sites.
<u>C</u>hildren chatter in busy playgrounds.
<u>D</u>ustbins doze on street corners.

Puzzling Word Pictures

In the series of word pictures on page 55 James Berry describes the *Workings of the Wind*. A number of the key verbs have been removed and can be found in a panel at the bottom of the page.

Reading the pictures

1 Read each of the 'pictures' carefully and choose the most 'fitting' word for each gap: e.g. 1 = shake.

2 Use the description and the other verbs used to help you. Work with a partner, discussing your choices. You may find you need to make several changes before you decide on your final list.

Workings of the Wind

Wind doesn't always topple trees
and ___1___ houses to pieces.

   Wind ___2___
   all over woods with weighty ghosts
   in swings in thousands,
   singing from every branch.

Wind doesn't always ___3___ windows
and push, push at walls.

   Wind ___4___
   down cul-de-sacs and ___5___
   dry leaves and old newspapers to leap
   and ___6___ like kite tails.

Wind doesn't always dry out
sweaty shirts and blouses.

   Wind ___7___
   pollen dust of flowers, washes
   people's and animals' faces
   and combs out birds' feathers.

Wind doesn't always ___8___ up waves
into white horses.

   Wind ___9___ up
   tree-shadows to dance on rivers,
   to ___10___ about on grass, and hanging
   lantern light to play signalman.

Wind doesn't always run wild
___11___ tinny dustbin lids.

   Wind makes
   leafy limbs ___12___ to red roses
   and ___13___ up and down outside windows
   and makes desk papers fly up indoors.

whistles	plays	bow
rattle	shake	scatters
whip	curl	bob
jig	worries	shakes
kicking		

Describing movement

As a class, see how many words you can come up with to describe the way something/ somebody can act or move. You can use a thesaurus to help you come up with ideas. Here are some to get you started:

   shuffle   prowl   sidle   bounce

Using your class word collection, each choose words to create two new word pictures to show:

- the way wind moves
- the way the wind does not move

Personification

In the following poem, the idea of the weather's movements is developed by describing the season of winter as though it is a person. We call it **personification** when an object or thing is described as though it were human.

Winter's character

As you listen to the poem read aloud, consider the kind of person you can see and hear being described.

- What clothes would this person wear?
- What would their hobbies be?
- What colour would their eyes/hair be?
- What would their voice sound like?
- What would their work be?
- Where would they live?

Winter

Winter crept
through the whispering wood
hushing fir and oak
crushed each leaf and froze each web
but never a word he spoke.

Winter prowled
by the shivering sea
lifting sand and stone;
nipped each limpet silently –
and then moved on.

Winter raced
down the frozen stream,
catching at his breath;
on his lips were icicles
at his back was death.

Judith Nicholls

Changing Winter's character

Try writing two more verses for this poem. Start by making a list of the verbs in the poem. (For more on verbs see pages 75–77 of Language Study.) Notice how carefully they are chosen so that we can picture this person clearly. Then use the guidelines below to help you.

1 Winter is something of a sinister character here. Do you want to continue this picture or do you want to give him/her a lighter face as was the case in *Workings of the Wind*?

2 Begin each verse with an action and place. You may want to consider these aspects of winter:
- icicles
- sunshine on ice
- light snow
- warm fires

3 Refer to 'Drafting a poem' on pages 49–51 for more advice and talk your ideas over with your teacher as you move from draft to draft.

Similes and Metaphors

Winter Morning

Snowflakes
for breakfast.
The street
outside
quiet
as
long
white
bandage.

Roger McGough

The Beach

The beach is a quarter of golden fruit
a soft ripe melon
sliced to a thick green rind
of jungle growth,
and the sea devours it
with its sharp
sharp white teeth.

William Hart-Smith

Using comparisons

A word picture will often use comparisons, as these two poems do, to bring a poet's ideas to life. The comparisons above are called similes and metaphors. A **simile** is a clear comparison that states one thing is like something else, using the words 'like' or 'as'. A **metaphor** can be harder to spot, but one object is described as though it *is* something else:

e.g. The beach is a quarter of golden fruit

See if you can explain just how the beach is similar to 'a quarter of golden fruit' by deciding what details would go in the centre column of the chart below. The chart for the comparison of snow to a bandage has already been completed to give you the idea.

Object	Similarity	Comparison
Snow	Colour	A bandage
	Covers what is usually there.	
	Muffles sound like a gag	

Object	Similarity	Comparison
A beach		A soft ripe melon
The sea		Sharp white teeth

Shakespeare's comparisons

In this next extract from *The Passionate Pilgrim*, Shakespeare looks at the difference between youth and the older generation, whom he calls 'age'. To make the contrast more vivid he uses comparisons to bring this to life: both similes and metaphors.

The first lines are laid out in the right order to introduce you to the style of the piece, but the later lines are jumbled. You need to sequence them in the right order, using the idea of contrast and comparison and the rhyme at the end of the lines to help you.

Crabbed Age and Youth

Crabbed Age and Youth
Cannot live together:
Youth is full of pleasance,
Age is full of care;
Youth like summer morn,
Age like winter weather

Youth is wild and Age is tame.
Age's breath is short;
Age is weak and cold,
Age like winter bare;
Youth is nimble, Age is lame;
Youth like summer brave,
Youth is full of sport,
Youth is hot and bold,

William Shakespeare

Taking it further

As you complete this, as a class see if you can add vivid comparisons to extend the poem. You could start by considering youth and age by their lifestyle:

e.g.   their clothes, contents of a handbag/ school bag/pocket, how they spend their spare time/their worries. Maybe you could make age sound more positive or youth harder?

These ideas could be a starting point:

Age is…pan stick, pink rinse and brave lipstick
Summer gloves and Sunday hats
Allotment trousers, scrubbed stiff with wire wool.

Poem as Sound

A World of Sound

Describing sounds

Can you imagine a world without sounds? That is what this poem does, but in doing so, it reminds us of the music around us in everyday life: the 'crunching', 'scraping', 'gurgling' of getting up in the morning!

Words which sound like the noise they describe, provide the poetic effect called **onomatopoeia** – a long word for a simple process.

Read this poem and enjoy all its noises. Then on your own, write out the words that sound like the noise they describe, e.g. 'whistling', 'purring'.

The Sound Collector

A stranger called this morning
Dressed all in black and grey
Put every sound into a bag
And carried them away

The whistling of the kettle
The turning of the lock
The purring of the kitten
The ticking of the clock

The popping of the toaster
The crunching of the flakes
When you spread the marmalade
The scraping noise it makes

The hissing of the frying-pan
The ticking of the grill
The bubbling of the bathtub
As it begins to fill

The drumming of the raindrops
On the window pane
When you do the washing up
The gurgling of the drain

The crying of the baby
The squeaking of the chair
The swishing of the curtain
The creaking of the stair

A stranger called this morning
He didn't leave his name
Left us only silence
Life will never be the same.

Roger McGough

Making a sound collage

As a class, pool the words you have found and use them to start a collection of 'sound words'. You could group these under headings such as:

- Sounds of Movement
- Sounds of Speech
- Sounds in the Kitchen

Each group could then be illustrated by a collage of pictures of the things connected with the sounds. The 'sound' words could then be stuck over the top on strips of paper.

Word collecting

It is not just sound words that are fun to collect, lots of words have a magic: words you say softly, words you say in your head, words you like to write, words you like to look at.

Make your own personal 'Word Collection'. As you come across good words add them to your list. Swap lists with friends. You could make a central class chart with everybody contributing their favourites.

Use this Judith Nicholls' poem to get your list started.

Wordhunter's Collection

There's wiggle and giggle
goggles and swatch,
straggle and gaggle
and toggle and itch.

Glimmering, shimmering,
glistening, twinkle,
poppycock, puddle
and muddle and pimple.

Peapod and flip-flop
rickety, dodo,
murmuring, lingering,
galaxy yo-yo.

Extra-terrestrial's
one that I love,
Betelgeuse, Pluto –
Heaven's above!

Who would not fall
for a bird called a chickadee?
A widgeon or warthog
or just a chimpanzee?

Many's the word
that I capture each day,
whispering each
till I know it will stay.

Judith Nicholls

Special sounds

Consider the sounds that are particularly special to you. Adrian Mitchell has begun to collect his special sounds below but the sounds and the objects that these refer to have been muddled up.

1 Use your own experience to match each sound to the action or object described.
  As you finish, read the piece aloud to yourself and add your own ideas to these lines paying particular attention to the sound words you choose.

Listening

The humble glistening song of	seals at play
Crackle and whisper of	the unicorn
The dragon roar of	a mountain stream
The heartbeat of	Christmas paper
Honking slapstick of	a factory
Pinecones rattling in	snails
Giggling pebbles in	a stormy tree
The silver hoofsteps of	the frosty stars

2 Pool your best ideas with the class to produce a class version of *Listening*.
  There is no limit to the number of versions you can come up with.

Sounds Strange

Unusual meanings

Have you any ideas about what these sound words could mean?

    Slubbery   scraith   hithery

They come from this poem which describes washing up using invented words.

    The 'skeleton' of this poem is printed below.

With a partner use:

- the sound of the word
- the events described
- and the rhyme

to decide into which line each word fits.

    e.g. 1 = scoopery

When you complete the poem, enjoy reading it aloud to hear the noisy process described.

Sink Song

Scouring out the porridge pot,
Round and round and round!

Out with all the scraith and ___1___
Lift the ___2___ ooly droopery
Chase the ___3___ slubbery gloopery
Round and round and round!

Out with all the ___4___ dithery
Ladle out the slimy ___5___
Hunt and catch the hithery ___6___
Round and round and round!

Out with all the obbly ___7___
On the stove it burns so bubbly
Use the spoon and use it doubly
Round and round and round!

J A Hendon

    scoopery   glubbery   gloopery
    eely   thithery   gubbly   slithery

Sound qualities

1 The sound of a word or phrase can make you think of different qualities. For example, 'droopery' is a very round, slow word whereas 'hithery' is a quick, sharp word.

Look at these two groups:

Slow, soft, warm, heavy, round	◄ In between ►	Quick, sharp, harsh, cold, light
Obbly		Thithery
Spoon		Hithery

With a partner, see if you can fit the nonsense words in *Sink Song* into one of these three columns. Make a list of them under the headings, only putting a word in the middle column if you are genuinely unsure.

2 Can you 'hear' these qualities of quickness, warmth, sharpness, etc in the sounds of the following extracts. As you read each one aloud, make your own notes about what the piece sounds like. The first is done for you.

In the hard-rutted lane
At every footstep breaks a brittle pane
And tinkling trees ice-bound ...

The snap and crackle of ice and frost is suggested by the harsh 'br' sound which is like shivering. Also the repeated 't' sound suggests music of icicles.

Hard Frost   *Andrew Young*

The bare black cliff clang'd round him, as he based
His feet on juts of slippery crag that rang
Sharp-smitten with the dint of armed heels

Tennyson   *Morte D'Arthur*

Gates snap like gunshot
as you handle them. Five-barred fragility ....

Winter-Piece   *Charles Tomlison*

Under my window, a clean rasping sound
When the spade sinks into gravelly ground

The cold smell of potato mould, the squelch and slap
of soggy peat, the curt cuts ....

Digging   *Seamus Heaney*

Experimenting with Sound

Bringing out the sounds

In a group of four, try reading this poem. You may want to repeat some words or to work in a round to echo some sounds.

You will need to practise your timing and practise your part carefully. Use the notes on page 42 to help you make notes around your poem first.

from *The Cataract of Lodore*

…Dividing and gliding and sliding,
And falling and brawling and sprawling,
And diving and riving and striving,
And sprinkling and twinkling and wrinkling,
And sounding and bounding and rounding,
And bubbling and troubling and doubling,
And grumbling and rumbling and tumbling,
And clattering and battering and shattering;
Retreating and beating and meeting and sheeting,
Delaying and straying and playing and spraying,
Advancing and prancing and glancing and dancing,
Recoiling, turmoiling and toiling and boiling,
And gleaming and streaming and steaming and beaming,
And rushing and flushing and brushing and gushing,
And flapping and rapping and clapping and slapping,
And curling and whirling and purling and twirling,
And thumping and plumping and bumping and jumping,
And dashing and flashing and splashing and clashing;
And so never ending, but always descending,
Sounds and motions for ever and ever are blending,
All at once and all o'er, with a mighty uproar,
And this way the Water comes down at Lodore.

Robert Southey

Taking it further

After your performance, stay in your groups and brainstorm as many action words as you can to describe one of the following:

■ the seaside   ■ a fairground   ■ a market place

When you have a large collection, try to link them by rhyming sounds, where the middle letters are the same, e.g. the 'sh' in 'dashing and flashing'. You could then link a performance of *The Cataract of Lodore* with a performance of your own poem.

Poem as Pattern
The Shape of Poetry

Poems can be written in any number of shapes. A quick flick through this module will show short poems, long poems, lines of equal length, irregular shapes and poems in a design of the object described.

Whatever their shape, though a writer will have chosen this carefully; the shape is part of the pattern of a poem.

Matching shape to meaning

In *The Fight of The Year*, Roger McGough describes the competition between winter and spring as one gives way to the other. *Ping-Pong* presents the excitement and action of the game it describes.

Read these pieces out loud with a partner and discuss why each poem takes its shape. Why are there long lines and short lines? Why are numbers used?

The pattern of the words helps us to 'see' the conflict, and the lack of punctuation helps us to feel the exhaustion of the events too!

The Fight of the Year

'And there goes the bell for the third month
and Winter comes out of his corner looking groggy
Spring leads with a left to the head
followed by a sharp right to the body
    daffodils
    primroses
    crocuses
    snowdrops
    lilacs
    violets
    pussy willow
Winter can't take much more punishment
and Spring shows no sign of tiring
    tadpoles
    squirrels
    baalambs
    badgers
    bunny rabbits
    mad March hares
    horses and hounds
Spring is merciless
Winter won't go the whole twelve rounds
    bobtail clouds
    scallywag winds
    the sun
    the pavement artist
    in every town
A left to the chin
and Winter's down!
    1 tomatoes
    2 radish
    3 cucumber
    4 onions
    5 beetroot
    6 celery
    7 and any
    8 amount
    9 of lettuce
    10 for dinner
Winter's out for the count
Spring is the winner!'

Roger McGough

Ping-Pong

Swatted between bats
The celluloid ball
Leaps on unseen elastic
Skimming the taut net.

Sliced
Screwed
Dabbed
                    Point
                    Service

Ping
Pong
Bing
Bong
                    Point
                    Service

Ding
Dong
Ting
Tang
                    Point
                    Service

Angled
Cut
Floated
Driven
            THWACKED
                Point

Spun
Cut
Smashed

Pong
Ping
Bong
Bing

Dong
Ding
Tong
Tong

Slipped
Driven
Caressed
Hammered

Bit
Tip
Slip
Zip
Whip

Left
Right
Twist
Skids
Eighteen
Eighteen
Nineteen
Nineteen
Twenty

Forehand
Swerves
Rockets
Battered
Cracked

                    Service

                    Point
                    Service

                    Point
                    Service

                        Point
                        Service

Smashed

Smashed

SMASHED

GAME

Bat
Tap
Slap
Zap
Whap

Yes
Yes
Yes
Yes
Seventeen
All
Eighteen
All
Nineteen

Backhand
Yes
Yes
Ah
Ah

Gareth Owen

Picture Poems

In the poems that follow the writers actually arrange their words to mirror the place, event or action they describe. Some are serious while others play with word size and shape to add humour and meaning.

Africa

THE SONG
THE BURNING SONG
THE DEMON VULTURES
THE HAZY TENTS   THE RAW
HORIZONS   THE DRUGGED SANDS   THE SCREAMING
THUNDER THE RATTLING BONES THE DUSTY MOUTHS
THE INFINITE EYES   THE DREAM POWER   THE CIRCLING
SKY   THE TREACHEROUS BIRDS THE SHIFTING TOWNS   THE
SNARLING GUNS THE BURNING STORM THE VAST RIVER THE
CLAY DANCERS   THE BLACK MASKS THE RICH SANDS THE HAZY
DEMON THE SCREAMING SKIES THE VULTURES MOUTHS THE RAW
EYES THE THUNDEROUS SONG THE SHIFTING TRACKS THE VAST
CIRCLE THE RATTLING BIRDS THE DUSTY TENTS THE GUNS SNARL
THE STEAMING HORIZON THE BONE FOREST THE BURNING TOWNS THE
SAND FLOWERS THE TREACHEROUS INFINITE THE BLACK TRACKED THE
DANCERS SCREAM THE MASKED GUNS THE THUNDERS MOUTH THE FOREST
TOWN THE CLAY HUTS THE STORMS POWER THE DRUGGED RIVER THE
SHIFTING SONGS THE SKYS EYE THE RATTLING DREAM THE SNARLING DUST THE
SANDS DEMONS THE BURNING BIRDS THE CIRCLING HAZE THE RAW BONES THE
RICH TENTS   THE SCREAMING FLOWER   THE STEAMING CLAY   THE BLACK SAND
THE MASKED   DANCE THE TREACHEROUS HORIZON THE STORMS TRACK
THE RIVER THUNDER   THE SHIFTY VULTURES   THE
FORESTS POWER   THE RAW SKY   THE SCREAMING
EYES   THE DREAM SONGS   THE DRUGGED HUTS
THE HAZY TOWNS   THE BURNT CIRCLE   THE
GUNS MOUTH   THE SNARLING BONES   THE
INFINITE BIRDS   THE DUSTY FLOWERS
THE STORMS MASK THE THUNDERING
DEMONS   THE TENT DANCERS   THE
RICH CLAY   THE SHIFTED POWER
THE SANDY RIVER   THE BURNING
TREACHERY   THE RATTLING TRACK
THE BLACK STEAM   THE POWERFUL
DREAM   THE FLOWERING SONG   THE
DRUGGED SCREAM THE DANCING EYE   THE
HORIZONTAL HUT THE MOUTHLESS   SNARLS
THE TRACKLESS SKY   THE RAW   FOREST
THE TENT TOWN   THE HAZY   RIVER
THE INFINITE SHIFT   THE   BIRD
STORM THE TREACHEROUS   DEMON
THE BURNING DRUG   THE   GUN
DANCE   THE SINGING
BONE   THE MASKED
RICH   THE BLACK
CIRCLING   THE
VAST DREAM
SINGING

Dave Calder

Grand Slam

Simon Hobbs

Creating an outline poem

Both *Grand Slam* and *Africa* use shape to carry their message.

1 In *Grand Slam* the words do not all follow in sentences but are all connected to the Five Nations Rugby Competition. A rugby ball forms the shape of the poem.
You can read the lines in any order and make different connections and stories. What 1995 Grand Slam stories are there in this poem?

Try writing your own newspaper poem.

- Collect newspapers and magazines
- Find a story that moves or interests you.
- Find an image or picture that sums up the story, e.g. heart for romance.
- Draw an outline shape.
- Go through the magazine and cut out words and phrases connected to your subject. Do not use pictures.
- Then arrange them in your shape.

Take your time to get it just as you want it.

2 In *Africa* the same idea is used but sets of short sentences are repeated and varied to create a dazzling word collage of the beauty and pain that is Africa.
Try this with a country of your choice. You could use Britain with the beauty of the natural world and the horror of pollution.

Words making shapes

1 *Wall Walk* makes your eyes follow the words as if you were actually balancing on top of the wall. Consider the shape and patterns of:

- playing hop scotch
- jumping downstairs
- climbing a tree

and try a shape poem of your own using one of these ideas.
Set out ideas, words, and sounds in patterns which mirror the actions.

2 What additional message does *Weekend in the Country* carry? Look particularly at the different type sizes used.

Wall Walk

THIN
WALL.
STEEP   FALL.
STEP
CARE-
FULLY
ARMS   OUT.
TIP   TIP
BUT
NOT
TOO
MUCH
TIP.
BAL-
ANCE
AH.
MADE IT.

Robert Froman

Weekend in the Country

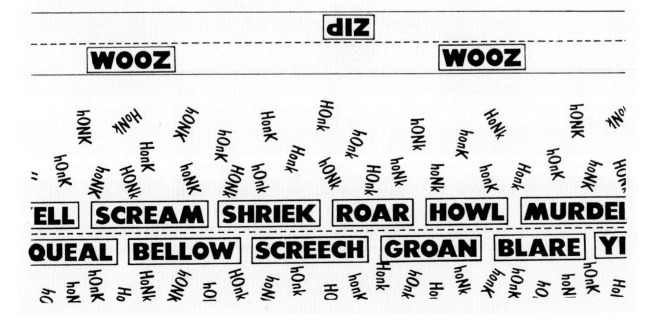

Robert Froman

3 As with *Weekend in the Country*, in these poems, the size and the arrangement of the words helps to convey a message:

■ big letters make a noise seem louder or an object closer

■ smaller letters seem quieter and make an object seem further away.

I Need Contact Lenses

John Hegley

Invasion

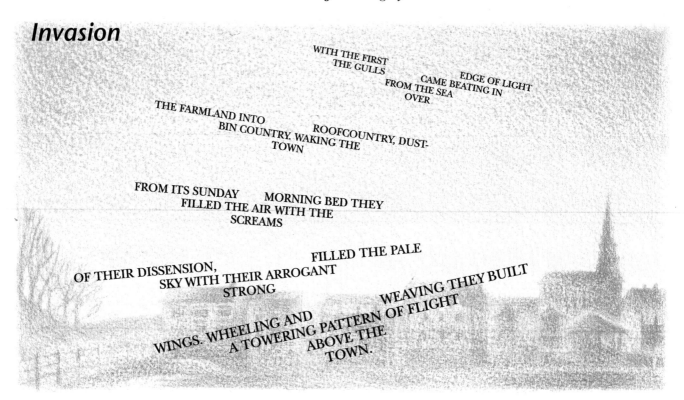

Pamela Gillilan

Shaping a poem

Using the ideas from *I Need Contact Lenses* and *Invasion*, arrange the words of the following Robert Froman poem, *Easy Diver*, into a shape that will show what is happening. Read the piece first. Then decide on a shape, and how you will use styles and sizes of lettering to put across the ideas in the poem. As you finish, compare your version with the original which your teacher will have a copy of.

Pigeon on the roof. Dives. Going fast. Going to hit hard!
Opens wings. Softly, gently, down.

Shaping Stories

Depicting a memory

In this poem, the writer has retold one boy's vivid childhood memory of bullying – including the voices, sounds, and actions that the event recalls. To make the story more dramatic he has:

- used a different print for words shouted out
- broken lines up to suggest the helter-skelter of the chase and his fragments of memory
- taken out punctuation to show how one memory slides into another
- shaped the lines about the ball to mirror a bouncing action

Johnny Nolan

Johnny Nolan has a patch on his ass

Kids chase him
　　　　　　through screendoor summers
Thru the back streets
　　　　　　of all my memories
Somewhere a man laments
　　　　　　upon a violin
A doorstep baby cries
　　　　　and cries again
　　　　like
　　　a
　　　　ball
　　　　　　bounced
　　　　　　　　down steps
Which helps the afternoon arise again
To a moment of remembered hysteria

Johnny Nolan has a patch on his ass

Kids chase him

Lawrence Ferlinghetti

Shaping the poem

The lines on page 73 are from a poem called *Who-man* which appears in a book of poems linked by ghostly and nightmarish happenings. In the original poem Philip Gross describes all the sinister masks that people can wear, e.g. armed robber's Balaclava, Hallowe'en mask, ghost costume. He looks at how it feels to someone looking at a masked figure.

On page 73 you have the poem all in one paragraph with no line breaks. With a partner, you are going to decide how to shape this poem.

1 Before you start, listen to the piece read aloud for you. (You may want to request further readings later, or try your own as you are working.)

2 Consider the following approaches that have been used in other poems in this unit. Then, design your own shape for the poem. You should be given a photocopy of the lines so you can chop them up and experiment with them.

- Decide where your line breaks are going to come.
- Will you have more than one voice in this poem? How will you show this?
- Will some lines be bold print and others softer?
- Will some words be larger/smaller than others?
- Will you use any capital letters for individual letters or words?
- Will some lines start in the middle or at the end of the page?

Include any other good ideas of your own. When you are ready, work together to write up your final version. Using a word processor may improve your presentation.

3 As you finish, ask your teacher for the original by Philip Gross and in your pair discuss which poem you prefer and why.

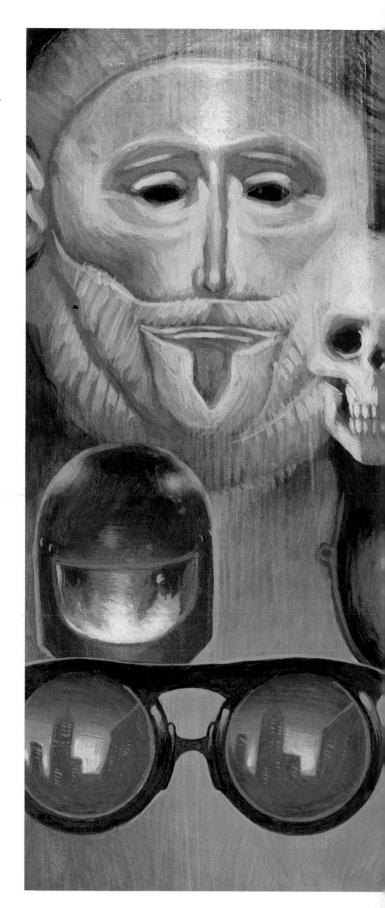

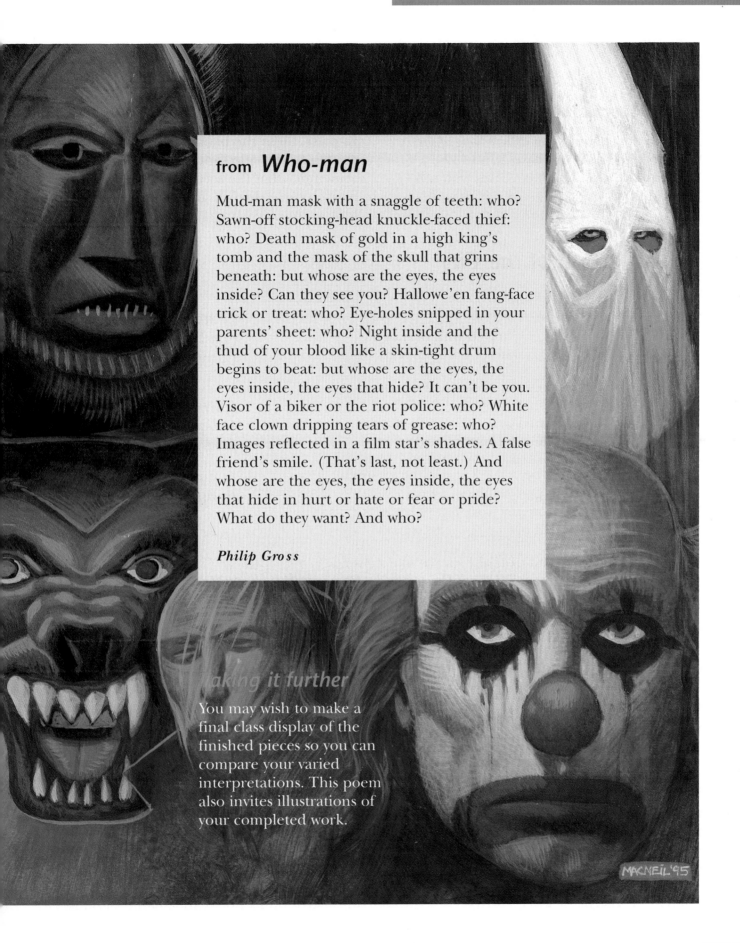

from *Who-man*

Mud-man mask with a snaggle of teeth: who?
Sawn-off stocking-head knuckle-faced thief:
who? Death mask of gold in a high king's
tomb and the mask of the skull that grins
beneath: but whose are the eyes, the eyes
inside? Can they see you? Hallowe'en fang-face
trick or treat: who? Eye-holes snipped in your
parents' sheet: who? Night inside and the
thud of your blood like a skin-tight drum
begins to beat: but whose are the eyes, the
eyes inside, the eyes that hide? It can't be you.
Visor of a biker or the riot police: who? White
face clown dripping tears of grease: who?
Images reflected in a film star's shades. A false
friend's smile. (That's last, not least.) And
whose are the eyes, the eyes inside, the eyes
that hide in hurt or hate or fear or pride?
What do they want? And who?

Philip Gross

Taking it further

You may wish to make a
final class display of the
finished pieces so you can
compare your varied
interpretations. This poem
also invites illustrations of
your completed work.

Language Study
Nouns

Which words fit?

Have you read the poem called *Song of the City* on page 52? If you have, this will be a memory exercise. If you have not, you will need to think carefully about which words will fit.

In pairs, fill in the blanks. There are clues written by the side (and it will help to remember that the second and fourth lines in each verse rhyme). If you need more help, look at the words marked by bullets below.

Song of the City

My brain is stiff with concrete
My limbs are rods of ___1___   (= metal)
My ___2___'s stuffed with money   (part of the body)
My ___3___ was bought in a deal.   ('body and -...?')

They poured metal through my arteries
They choked my ___4___ with lead   (parts of the body)
They churned my ___5___ to plastic   (a liquid)
They put murder in my ___6___.   (= mind)

I'd a face like a ___7___ of the weather   (a diagram)
Flesh that grew to the ___8___   (body substance)
But they tore my story out of my eyes
And turned my ___9___ to stone.   (part of the body)

Let me wind from my source like a river
Let me grow like wheat from the ___10___   ('wheat-seed')
Let me hold out my ___11___ like a natural tree (parts of the body)
Let my ___12___ love me again.   (= people)

Gareth Owen

Common nouns and proper nouns

The words missed out are obviously very important to the meaning. Each of them was a word for a person (or people) or a thing (or things). Choose from this list.

- People: children
- Things: steel, soul, bone, lungs, blood, arms, grain, belly, head, heart, map

On page 36, you learned about proper nouns which label particular people, places or things. These always begin with a capital letter.

In *Song of the City* the children in the final line are not given particular names: they are labelled simply as 'children'. We call this kind of word a **common noun**. All the other words missed out of the poem are in fact common nouns too.

Look back at the complete poem on page 52. Which other words are common nouns?

Verbs

Verbs are the words which enable us to say what people or things are doing (or being) in a sentence.

Verbs of action

On page 57 you were asked to pick out the verbs in Judith Nicholls' poem, *Winter*. You might have listed the following:

crept, crushed, froze, spoke, prowled, nipped, moved, raced.

It is easy to see that these are verbs, because they all label some kind of action. You might even have learnt to call verbs 'doing words'.
In another activity, on page 55, there is a list of verbs to place into the gaps in James Berry's poem, *Workings of the Wind*. These are all verbs of action:

whistles, plays, bow, rattle, shake, scatters... etc.

Verbs of being

Many of the commonest verbs, though, can hardly be called 'actions' at all. They label the way we are or feel or become. In *Winter* you will find two examples of the commonest verb of this kind:

...on his lips *were* icicles
at his back *was* death.

Look back at John Mole's poem, *The Shoes*, on page 48. List the verbs in the first eight lines, saying which ones are *verbs of being* and which *verbs of action*.

Changing the verbs

To see how important verbs are to the meaning of a sentence, try changing them. Most of Robert Southey's poem, *The Cataract of Lodore* is made up of verbs joined by the word 'and':

e.g. Dividing and gliding and sliding...

After that poem on page 65, you were asked to create your own poem, based on Southey's, using as many action words as you could think up. The following verbs might help you to write a poem about one of the choices given there – a market place.

Find one or two verbs which rhyme with each one in this list. Then use as many as possible as a basis for your poem like Southey's:

buying	spending	looking	cheeping
saying	sending	lifting	heaping
calling	saving	cheating	shopping
talking	arriving	picking	stealing
bustling	ringing	greeting	packing

Adverbs

In Judith Nicholls' poem on page 56, Winter '...nipped each limpet silently'. Because the word 'silently' tells us something about the verb 'nipped', we call it an **adverb**.

Adding adverbs

An adverb can help a verb by providing more information and enabling the reader to gain a clearer picture. To see this in action, add three different adverbs to each of the following verbs. (One adverb has been added in each case to start you off.)

- He talked *quietly* to his friend.
- They walked *slowly* through the crowd.
- I thought about it *carefully* for a few minutes.

Doing without adverbs

In each of the examples above, we could have chosen a single verb to replace the verb plus adverb combination. For example:

- He whispered to his friend.
- They strolled through the crowd.
- I considered it for a few minutes.

With a partner, turn to page 65 and decide which carefully chosen verbs Southey has included in his poem, *The Cataract of Lodore*, instead of these rather long-winded (and less precise) combinations of verb plus adverb.

line 1:   flying smoothly
line 3:   trying hard
line 5:   jumping springily
line 8:   hitting hard
line 12: working hard
line 13: shining brightly
line 16: spinning quickly
line 19: moving downwards
line 20: mixing together

Word Classes

Nouns, verbs, adjectives, and adverbs all perform different jobs in a sentence. They are known as **word classes**.

Where English Words Come From

Old English

Have you ever wondered where English words come from?

Most of the commonest words in English come from a language called Old English, which was spoken a thousand years ago.

For example, the poem, *Wordhunter's Collection* on page 61, contains dozens of exciting and unusual words. But the lines:

Who would not fall
for a bird called a chickadee?

contain only one word which is not from Old English. (Which one, do you think? How can you guess?)

Old English was brought over to our shores by the Angles and Saxons who settled here after the Fifth century, and so it is sometimes called Anglo-Saxon.

Borrowing

Although the English language we speak today is mainly based upon Old English, it has always grown by **borrowing** words from other languages. And we have only to look back at Judith Nicholls' poem, *Wordhunter's Collection*, to get an idea of the many languages which have helped to build what we now know as 'English'. The study of word origins is called **etymology**.

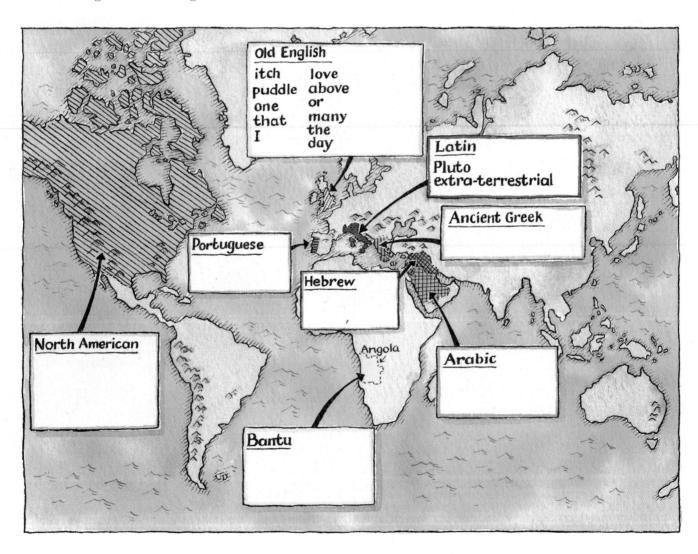

Old English
itch   love
puddle   above
one   or
that   many
I   the
  day

Latin
Pluto
extra-terrestrial

Ancient Greek

Portuguese

Hebrew

North American

Angola

Arabic

Bantu

Wordhunting on the map

A number of the words from Judith Nicholls' poem have been placed on the map according to the area of the world they originally came from.

1   Fill in the empty boxes when you have completed questions 1 and 2 in 'Taking it further' below. You will be given your own copy of the map.

2   Add some more examples of words in the poem that come from Old English.

Taking it further

1   Use a dictionary and the map to help you find where these words come from. They are all in *Wordhunter's Collection* (except one which is the poet's first name):

   ■ 'Judith' (Clue: the name is in the Bible, and comes from the area now called Israel.)
   ■ 'capture' (Clue: the Romans spoke this language.)
   ■ 'and' (Clue: it is one of our commonest words.)

2   Which word do you think:

   ■ comes from a West African language
   ■ comes from North American English
   ■ comes from Arabic? (Clue: many names of stars are Arabic.)

3   Why do you think

   ■ 'dodo' might come from the Portuguese word for 'a fool'
   ■ 'galaxy' might come from a word meaning 'milky' in Ancient Greek
   ■ 'rickety' might come from the name for the disease 'rickets'?

4   How do you think the words 'giggle', 'flip-flop', and 'murmur' were invented? (Clue: there are other examples of words like this on pages 60–61 of the Poetry module.)
   Why do you think people would call a bird a 'chickadee'? (Clue: think of cuckoo.)

5   All of the words in this phrase come from the same language:

   ...whispering each
   till I know it will stay.

   Which language? How could you guess?

6   'Extra-terrestrial' is from Latin, the language of the Romans. The word comes from the Latin *extra*, meaning 'outside' and *terra*, meaning 'land'. Find out what 'Mediterranean' means.

Giving Information

Looking at Reading Habits

What types of books do most people have in their homes? Do you think people have mostly fiction books, such as novels, poetry, plays, etc or non-fiction, such as encyclopedias, telephone directories, car manuals, etc?

Favourite books

Look at this list of types or genres of books. In a survey of British homes in 1994, people were asked which of these books they had.

1 In groups of four, put the books into an order of most popular to least popular from 1 to 13. Then decide how many homes you think have no books.

> Bible
> Car repair manual
> Cookery book
> DIY manual
> Encyclopedia
> English dictionary
> First aid manual
> Foreign language dictionary
> Gardening/indoor plant book
> Local street guide
> Medical dictionary
> Road atlas – GB
> World atlas
> no books

2 What do you think are the favourite types of books which people in Britain buy from bookshops? Look at these two lists of men's and women's book-buying habits and try again to place them in rank order.

Women		Men	
	Baby and childcare		Car repair manual
	Classics/literature		Computer manual
	Cookery book		Cookery book
	Crime/thriller		Crime/thriller
	Diet/health		Gardening
	Food/drink		Puzzle/quiz book
	Gardening/plants		Science fiction
	Historical novel		Sports/games instructions
	Puzzle/quiz book		Sports/games non-fiction
	Romance		War/adventure

3 Before you look at the answers for both surveys, discuss the decisions you have made and how you reached them. Think also about types of books which are *not* listed here which you might have expected to be. Then look at the results boxes below.

Survey results

Part 1: Books in British Homes

The list of books in order of popularity is:

1	English dictionary	87%
2	Cookery book	77%
3	Bible	60%
4	Road atlas	57%
5	Gardening/indoor plants	55%
6	Car repair manual	50%
7	Local street guide	49%
8	DIY manual	44%
8	Encyclopedia	44%
10	World atlas	38%
11	Foreign language dictionary	37%
12	Medical dictionary	32%
13	First aid manual	30%
	No books	1%

(%s show the number of households possessing each type of book.)

Books and the Consumer, 1994

Part 2: Women's and Men's Reading Tastes

The results show which books people of both sexes buy most. They are listed in rank order, i.e. the most popular book is at number one.

WOMEN
1 Cookery book
2 Romance
3 Crime/thriller
4 Puzzle/quiz book
4 Gardening/plants
6 Food/drink
6 Historical novel
8 Classics/literature
8 Baby and childcare
10 Diet/health

MEN
1 Crime/thriller
2 Car repair manual
3 Cookery book
4 Computer manual
4 Gardening
4 Sports/games non-fiction
7 Sports/games instructions
8 War/adventure
9 Science fiction
10 Puzzle/quiz book

Books and the Consumer, 1994

Discussing the results

In your group discuss the following points and make notes of your conclusions to share with the rest of the class.

1 For each list, decide which of the categories is fiction; which is non-fiction?

2 Compare each set of survey results with your predictions. What did you get right and wrong?

3 Which result do you find most surprising?

4 What would seem to be the main differences between the reading habits of women and men?

5 Which of the books do all the members of your discussion group have at home? Which do none of the group own?

Taking it further

Write a 'Reading Autobiography', which describes the five books which have made the most impact on you during your life. Try to choose books from across a range of years. Describe them, saying what you remember about when and where you read them, and discuss why they have proved so memorable. Try to cover non-fiction (reference books, manuals) as well as fiction books.

Instructions

Give and take

How good are you at giving instructions? Do you listen well when you receive instructions? Find out by trying this experiment.

Work in a group of three, with two sitting back-to-back. One of you should give instructions (person **A**); another should follow them (person **B**). The third (person **C**) is the observer.

Person A: without watching, give **B** instructions about how to put on and tie a school tie.

Person B: follow **A**'s instructions exactly. Imagine that you know nothing at all about how to put on a tie. The only information you have is from **A**'s guidance.

Person C: should watch and make notes on how the instructions given could be clearer.

Allow three minutes for the activity. At the end of this, **C** should give as many positive suggestions for improving the giving and receiving of instructions as possible.

Bike advice

Now look at some written instructions. This extract from the *Usborne Book of Bikes* gives instructions on how to repair a puncture.

How clear do you find the instructions for this process?

- Look at the information contained in the extract. Is there enough detail or too little?
- Is the language simple enough or too simple? How do the short sentences that are used help the clarity of the instructions? Look in particular at how each sentence starts with a direction to do something, e.g. in paragraph 2 'Remove... Listen... Mark....'
- How well do the the illustrations match the written explanations?
- How do these written instructions compare with the spoken ones you devised for putting on the tie.

Emergency repair: Punctures

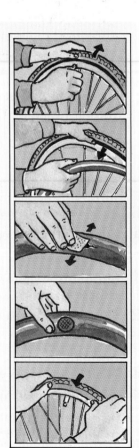

1. Remove the wheel (see page 41). Now, starting opposite the valve, remove one side of the tyre from the rim.

2. Remove the inner tube then inflate it. Listen for a hiss or put the tyre in water and watch for bubbles. Mark the hole.

3. Use fine sandpaper to roughen area around the hole. Blow away any dust. Spread glue on the area. Leave for two minutes.

4. Stick on the patch then let it dry for three minutes. Check in the tyre for grit.

5. Starting with the valve, replace the tube, then the tyre, on the rim. Make sure it is tucked in all the way. Pump up the tyre.

Usborne Book of Bikes

Mad scramble

1 Now look at these disorganized instructions. Read them through and sort them into the correct order, by writing down the paragraph numbers in the order that you think is the right one, like this:

   Para 1 = 3

Cleaning Teeth

1 As you brush, make sure that you are cleaning your gums as well as your teeth. Gentle brushing strengthens gums and makes you less likely to develop gum problems later in life.

2 Cleaning your teeth in this way will take around two minutes. You should do it at least twice a day, ideally after meals.

3 First, choose your toothbrush wisely. One that is too hard will make your gums bleed. An electric plaque-remover is a very good way to keep your teeth and gums healthy because it reaches all parts of the mouth.

4 Repeat the process with the bottom teeth.

5 Put a small amount of toothpaste onto the toothbrush – about a centimetre will be fine.

6 When you have finished brushing, swill out your mouth with water. Then rinse the toothbrush and put it away. Your teeth should now be cleaner and have a better chance of staying healthy.

7 Next open your mouth and begin to brush at the top left-hand side, starting with the backs of the teeth, working round to the top right-hand side. Then do the front of all your top teeth.

2 Once you have decided upon the correct order, compare it with a partner's. Then look again at the instructions and pick out eight different words or phrases which helped you to reorganize them – like this:

Words	How they helped to reorganize the text
First...	Hinted that this was the opening instruction
in this way...	
Next...	
Then...	

3 Write your own set of scrambled instructions for one of these processes and swap them with your partner to see if they can unscramble them.
   - Making tea
   - Making a telephone call from a public phone box
   - Cleaning shoes

Hazard House

One of the times when making instructions clear is most important is when you give someone directions. Below is a map of Hazard House – a house containing hidden treasure. A gang of smugglers stashed it there before they were caught. To stop people from getting hold of their riches, they booby-trapped the house, leaving it full of hazards for anyone trying to recover the treasure.

Your mission

Working in pairs, your mission is to help retrieve the treasure by avoiding the hazards. You have only 5 minutes to do this.

1 Your partner is at the delivery entrance with a walkie-talkie. You are back at base with the colour plan of the house. Direct your partner through the house to the treasure and out of the back door. Use instructions like this:

> Go straight ahead until you reach a door. Turn left…

Warn your partner about the hazards they will encounter, so that they can be prepared for them.

2 As you give your instructions, your partner should trace the progress they make on an outline plan.

3 As you complete the mission, discuss any other routes you might have taken or how your instructions might have been better.

Taking it further

1 Imagine you are seeking the hidden treasure alone. You are in Hazard House with only a torch and the plan. Write a story showing what happens to you and describing in detail the route you take.

2 Design your own plan or map – of a cave, an island, or a haunted house. Then write a story describing an adventure you have there. Include an account of the route you take as you travel around and the hazards you successfully avoid.

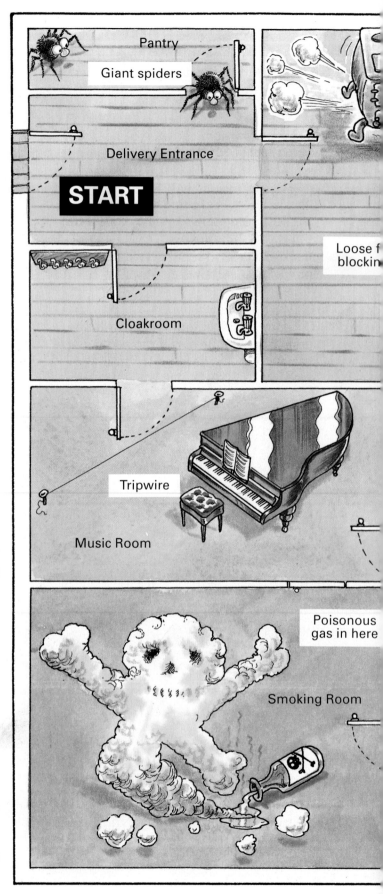

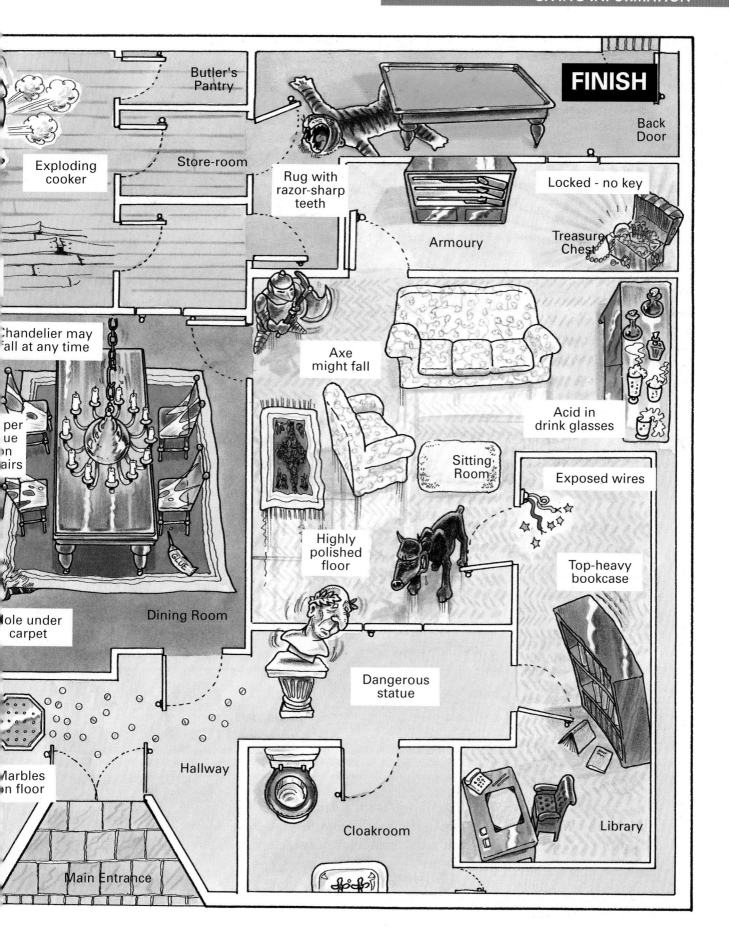

The Knowledge Challenge

Dr Johnson was a writer in the Eighteenth century. He is especially well known for compiling one of the first dictionaries. According to Dr Johnson, if you are not knowledgeable yourself, then you need to know where to find information ...

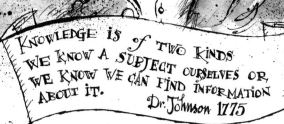

KNOWLEDGE IS of TWO KINDS WE KNOW A SUBJECT OURSELVES OR, WE KNOW WE CAN FIND INFORMATION ABOUT IT. Dr. Johnson 1775

Just a minute

Which subjects are you knowledgeable about? What are you an expert in? For example, can you talk without saying 'er' and 'um' for a minute on one of these topics:

- a sport or hobby
- computers
- a pet
- a famous person
- an important event in history

Where to look

1 Write down the list of subjects below. Against each one make a note of where you would seek information about it. If you can think of better sources than those listed, write down your own ideas.

Information needed about	Source of information
1 The next bus into town	Friend/relative
2 Facts about woodlice	Reference book
3 Recipe for chocolate-chip cookies	Telephone directory
4 How to fly a kite	Noticeboard
5 Today's temperature	Library
6 The date of the Battle of Agincourt	Specialist book
7 What someone in your class really thinks about someone else	Newspaper
	Timetable
8 The phone number of a reliable plumber	Computer database
	TV programme
	Magazine

2 When is it more suitable to ask someone for information, and when is it better to use a written source, e.g. a book or computer database? Make some notes on the advantages and disadvantages of using spoken or written forms of information.

> Asking someone for information might be better when…
>
> Written sources of information might be better when…

Three sources

Now read these three sources of information on the subject of 'Diving'. These are taken from:

■ a magazine information feature
■ an encyclopedia
■ a children's encyclopedia

Divers

Divers may go beneath the surface of the sea for a number of reasons: to assist in building docks, repairing oil rigs, salvaging ships, or perhaps just to explore the sea-bed.

The simplest form of diving is to fill your lungs with air by taking a deep breath and then dive as deep as you can. Unassisted diving like this allows you to stay below for no more than about 2 minutes and to reach a depth of about 10 m (30 ft).

To stay down longer or go deeper you must be supplied with oxygen or air, which, of course, contains oxygen. The ordinary diver's suit is made of rubber and has a metal helmet with a glass window in it. A pump on the surface forces air down a pipe connected to the diver's suit and allows fresh air to be breathed.

The stale air which the diver breathes out escapes from the suit and bubbles up to the surface. With a suit like this, a diver can go down to about 60 m (200 ft). With an aqualung, a diver uses a mask to breathe oxygen directly from bottles carried on the back. There is no need for an air line to the surface, so the diver can swim around much more easily.

The deeper divers go the greater the pressure of water, and the more the nitrogen in the air they breathe dissolves in the blood. When this happens divers must come up very slowly or the nitrogen will form

bubbles in the blood rather like the bubbles you see when you take the top off a lemonade bottle. This effect is very painful and is called 'the bends'. It is very dangerous, and if divers come up too quickly it will kill them.

Flashback

The type of diving suit with metal helmet and air line was designed by Siebe in 1830 and is still in use. In World War II many navies used 'frogmen' who carried their own air in bottles on their backs and wore flippers on their feet. When divers today have to go to a great depth they breathe a mixture of oxygen and a special gas called helium which has the strange effect of making their voices sound squeaky. ■

▲ Scuba diver equipped with camera and flash unit, in the Red Sea, Israel.

SCUBA divers are divers who carry their own air supply with them in aqualungs. **S**elf **C**ontained **U**nderwater **B**reathing **A**pparatus.

Scuba divers have reached depths of over 130 m.

People have dived over 80 m just holding their breath, but deep diving like this is extremely dangerous.

DIVING
WORKING & EXPLORING UNDERWATER

ANCIENT AQUALUNG
THE ANCIENT ASSYRIANS (c1500BC) SWAM UNDERWATER FOR UP TO 20 MINUTES BY BREATHING FROM GOAT SKINS FULL OF AIR.

THE DIVING BELL
THE ASTRONOMER, SIR EDMUND HALLEY, PERFECTED THE DIVING BELL IN 1706.
LEAD-LINED BARRELS OF AIR DROPPED FROM THE SURFACE TO REPLENISH AIR IN BELL.
HALLEY'S CAP OF MAINTENANCE, THE PREDECESSOR OF THE HELMET

A NATURAL DIVING BELL
THE WATER SPIDER CREATES BELL-SHAPED CHAMBER OF SILK ANCHORED TO WATERWEEDS. THIS IT FILLS WITH AIR BY REPEATEDLY SWIMMING DEEPER & RELEASING AIR TRAPPED UNDER ITS HAIRY BODY INTO THE BELL.

A NATURAL SNORKEL
SOME AIR INSECTS BREED UNDERWATER, DRAWING THEIR AIR THROUGH THE HOLLOW STEMS OF WATER LILIES BY USING THEM AS SNORKELS.

THE DIVER
THE EARLIEST HELMETS WERE NOT SEALED TO A SUIT AT THE NECK & FILLED WITH WATER IF THE DIVER FELL.
DIVER ADJUSTS EXHAUST VALVE TO ALTER VOLUME OF AIR IN SUIT & HENCE HIS BUOYANCY.
18 KG + 18 KG ON BACK
8 KG

THE BENDS
AS A DIVER DESCENDS, THE PRESSURE INSIDE HIS BODY INCREASES & HIS BLOOD TAKES UP MORE & MORE NITROGEN FROM THE AIR.
FIZZO FIZZO FIZZO
WHEN THE DIVER RISES TOO FAST, NITROGEN BUBBLES APPEAR IN THE BLOOD (JUST LIKE THE BUBBLES WHICH FORM WHEN A FIZZY DRINK BOTTLE IS OPENED & PRESSURE IS REDUCED). THE NITROGEN BUBBLES CREATE CRAMPS & OTHER SYMPTOMS CALLED THE BENDS.

DEEP-SEA BREATHING
DIVERS CAN GO MUCH DEEPER BY BREATING A MIXTURE OF HELIUM, NITROGEN & OXYGEN THAN BY BREATHING AIR. HELIUM DOES NOT DISSOLVE SO READILY IN THE BLOOD & BEING LIGHTER, DIFFUSES OUT QUICKER — MAKING THE BENDS LESS LIKELY.

WETSUITS
WETSUITS ARE CLOSE-FITTING BUT NOT WATERTIGHT. WATER SEEPS IN, BECOMES TRAPPED & QUICKLY WARMS UP. THE AIR BUBBLES IN THE FOAM MATERIAL ACT AS AN INSULATOR.
AS THE DIVER DESCENDS, THE FOAM BUBBLES ARE COMPRESSED, REDUCING HIS BUOYANCY. A DIVER WHO FLOATS AT SURFACE LEVEL MAY SINK AT 50m BELOW.

DRYSUITS
DRYSUITS ARE SEALED AT WRISTS & ANKLES TO KEEP THE DIVER DRY & CAN BE WORN WITH WARM UNDERWEAR.
AS THE DIVER DESCENDS, ANY RESIDUAL AIR IN THE SUIT IS COMPRESSED & CREASES BECOME RIGID, PINCHING THE SKIN & HAMPERING MOVEMENT. THESE SUITS ARE ONLY WORN WHEN WORKING IN POLLUTED OR VERY COLD WATER.

LUXURY SUITS
SOME EXPENSIVE WETSUITS USE MILLIONS OF TINY SEALED BUBBLES OF GLASS INSTEAD OF FOAM. THESE ARE INCOMPRESSIBLE & KEEP THE BUOYANCY CONSTANT.

HOW TO STOP WRITING FROM RUNNING WHEN WET
SIMPLY RUB A CANDLE THOROUGHLY OVER THE WRITING.

---

diving sport of entering water either from a springboard (3 m/10 ft) above the water, or from a platform, or highboard, (10 m/33 ft) above the water. Various starts are adopted, and twists and somersaults may be performed in mid-air. Points are awarded and the level of difficulty of each dive is used as a multiplying factor.

diving apparatus any equipment used to enable a person to spend time underwater. Diving bells were in use in the 18th century, the diver breathing air trapped in a bell-shaped chamber. This was followed by cumbersome diving suits in the early 19th century. Complete freedom of movement came with the ⇨ aqualung, invented by Jacques ⇨ Cousteau in the early 1940s. For work at greater depths the technique of saturation diving was developed in the 1970s by which divers live for a week or more breathing a mixture of helium and oxygen at the pressure existing on the seabed where they work (as in tunnel building).

Tim Hunkin

1 Working in groups of four, see what differences you notice in:
- the information given to you in each source
- the way this information is presented.

2 Use these discussion points to compare the three sources.
- Which text did you find most interesting - why?
- Which had the most difficult language?

Pick out some examples to support your ideas.

- Which text (A, B or C) would be best for...

...someone who wants to know technical details about diving?

...someone who isn't really interested in the subject?

...someone who wants to write a project on diving?

...someone who just wants a brief outline of the subject?

3 Taking the ideas from your discussion, decide which text is which? How can you tell?

Taking it further

1 Choose a subject which you are interested in, and present it in the style of a Tim Hunkin illustrated fact page. You might choose a hobby, a favourite topic, a type of sport or music, a place you have visited, or someone you admire.

First create a draft of the layout, placing different pieces of information in separate sections. Try to finish with a 'How to...' section, as Tim Hunkin does. Then check your work and produce a finished version.

2 Information is often stored on computer. On the video, watch how two Year 7 students find out information about diving using a CD-ROM.

As a class, discuss the advantages and disadvantages of storing information in this way.

Persuading People

Holiday Ahoy

Holidays on TV

How are people persuaded to choose a particular place for their holiday?

1 Have a look at the TV holiday commercial on the video and discuss how it tries to make viewers want to buy a particular holiday. Give the commercial a star rating to show how much it makes you want to go on a holiday with that firm:

> Star rating
> * = not at all
> ** = quite like to go
> *** = would love to go

Then discuss these points in a group of four.

- Who you think the commercial is aimed at? Which age groups? How can you tell?
- What impression of the types of holiday on offer do the words and pictures create?
- How is music used to add to the effect?
- What is the effect of including a TV celebrity in the commercial?

2 Now watch the extract from the BBC's *Holiday* programme. In this report actress, Maureen Lipman, and her mother visit the seaside resort of Southwold. Their aim here is chiefly to inform the viewer about Southwold but do they also persuade them either to go there or to avoid it? In your group, discuss these questions:

- What impression do the presenters give of the place?
- What is their attitude to what they see?
- How much do they make you want to go there? Use the star rating system again.

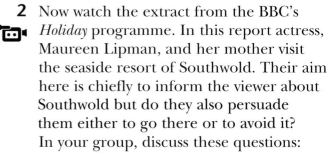

Lunn Poly WHERE AN IDENTICAL HOLIDAY CAN COST YOU **25%** LESS.

Choosing from a brochure

How do travel companies persuade readers that they should book a holiday with them?

With a partner, look at the holiday brochures shown here and on page 92. These are for two very different types of holiday.

How do the brochures use layout and language to persuade readers that 'this' is the holiday for them?

To help you compare the brochures, follow the steps given on page 93.

Hoseasons holiday brochure

Treat yourself to a boating holiday to find out what you've been missing

A WATERBORNE HOLIDAY *in Britain is an inspired choice for a decidedly different time away. It's so relaxing, so utterly different from the everyday world, so friendly, so much fun for children — truly a 'get away from it all' break with a captivating atmosphere all its own.*

THE VARIED ATTRACTIONS *of boating appeal to every age group and it's the kind of holiday which gives everyone a chance to join in, try something new and have a lot of fun into the bargain.*

HOSEASONS' CHOICE *of waterways have been carefully selected to provide not only a variety of boating experiences but also a leisurely freedom to discover new aspects of Britain.*

ALONG THE WINDING RIVERS *and canals which weave through some of the loveliest areas of England, Scotland and Wales you're free to decide each day exactly what to do and when. Free to cruise along picturesque waterways at a gentle pace and free to go ashore to explore countryside, villages, castles, manors and historic towns.*

ABOVE

Cruising the beautiful Caldon Canal, Staffordshire

RIGHT

Peace and tranquillity at Oulton Broad on the Norfolk Broads

> 66
> *BEING AFLOAT GIVES AN EXTRA TOUCH OF FREEDOM TO A SELF CATERING HOLIDAY*
> 99

News of the World, February 1993

YOU'LL ALSO MEET *a lot of friendly people, particularly at locks and moorings, all happy to swap tips on what to do and where to go. There'll be opportunities galore to fish, swim, cycle and ramble in search of flowers, birds and wildlife. Plenty of occasions too when you'll spy a delightful waterside inn or restaurant and decide it's the perfect place to stop for a while or moor for the night and enjoy dinner ashore.*

IF YOU'RE NEW TO BOATING *you'll quickly pick up the ropes from the helpful staff at your Hoseasons boatyard and when you feel confident you can cast off and look forward to a carefree cruise. All Hoseasons' boats are easy to handle, well maintained and thoughtfully equipped to ensure comfortable living on board.*

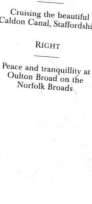

Entertainment Florida style

BRITISH AIRWAYS HOLIDAYS

Themed 'attractions' are as American as apple pie! Some, like Florida's Busch Gardens, specialise in thrills – with roller coasters that reach breakneck speeds ... Others, like Church Street Station in Orlando's restored downtown area, take you back to the good ol' days of saloon bar America through its shops, restaurants and evening shows... Make it in the movies at Universal Studios or enter the gentler surrounds of Sea World where rare species are protected through vital captive breeding and conservation programmes.

Wet 'n Wild

'Surf's up' at Wet 'n Wild. You can 'catch' 4 ft waves at Surf Lagoon, 'go for a spin' on the Ragin' Rapids or plunge the 76ft 'freefall' of Der Stuke. The watery possibilities here are endless.

Cypress Gardens

More impressive each year, Florida's very first theme park offers 8,000 varieties of beautifully planted tropical gardens, the world's famous Cypress Gardens waterski team, as well as the Gardens' newest attraction – Wings of Wonder Butterfly Conservatory.

Church Street Station

Downtown Orlando's complete entertainment, dining and shopping complex, Church Street Station offers you the choice of Dixieland Jazz at the legendary 'Rosie O' Grady's, Country and Western, Rock & Roll – plus more besides.

Universal Studios

Visit Hollywood in Florida at Universal Studios - the largest working studio complex outside of 'Tinsel Town' itself. 'Ride the Movies' with King Kong, and the Ghostbusters team, take a bike ride with a difference in the ET Adventure or Blast 'Back to the Future' courtesy of Doc Brown ... and don't miss 'Jaws', Universal Studio's latest attraction.

Kennedy Space Center

Live the dream of manned space exploration at the Kennedy Space Center. See the launch site for the Space Shuttle and many of the Apollo lunar missions, plus an array of rockets, lunar rovers and landers – even a space shuttle itself.

Sea World

As oceans become more polluted and natural habitat continues to be lost, the conservation work carried out by Sea World becomes more important by the day. See threatened species such as the Florida manatee, giant sea turtles, sharks and dolphins – not forgetting 'Shamu' the killer whale – and learn more about the fascinating undersea world and how we can protect it.

Busch Gardens

Turn upside down seven times on Busch Gardens' 60 mph 'Kumba' - the largest and fastest steel roller coaster in the southeastern United States! The 'Scorpion' and 'Python' offer even more thrills and excitement. At a gentler pace explore some 300 acres of grounds, where more than 3,400 animals live in the open – including chimps, gorillas, lions and giraffe.

British Airways brochure

Pictures

1 Compare the pictures used in both brochures. What impression do they give of the holiday? Use these words and phrases to help you describe what the pictures are saying:

fun   back to nature
for family   scientific
educational   active
relaxing   unpredictable
exciting

2 Look at the way the pictures are presented. Why do some have straight edges and others seem like cut-outs? What effect does this have?

Headings

3 Look at the headings that are used in both brochures. What do you notice about:
■ the number of headings used
■ the styles of type used
■ the words used in the headings?
Which advertisement do you think is more attractive, and why?

Text

4 Now compare the writing in both brochures. Look at this panel of descriptive words from the first part of each brochure. How are they different in the impression they give?

Descriptive words about...

Hoseasons

decidedly different

utterly different

relaxing

captivating atmosphere

Florida

as American as apple pie

breakneck speeds

good ol' days

saloon bar America

5 Who do you think is the audience for each brochure? Are they
    male/female
    single/family
    young/middle-aged/older?
What clues can you find in the texts to support your ideas?

6 Write up your notes into a brief report about the two brochures, or discuss your findings with the rest of the class.

Taking it further

Now think about the area you live in. Either produce a holiday brochure, or the script of a report for BBC TV's *Holiday*. Start by making a list of the area's attractions. Then decide how you would persuade people to visit.

Holiday Challenge

Mr and Mrs Trotter are the most miserable couple on Earth. They hate the idea of holidays. They think they cost a fortune; that their luggage will go missing; that they will be surrounded by people they do not like; that they will return home with mysterious illnesses...

Could you persuade this couple that what they really need is a holiday?

Persuading the Trotters

1 In pairs, role play a conversation in which Mr and Mrs Trotter discuss why they dislike the idea of holidays so much. Perhaps they went on holiday once, long in the past, and that put them off for life.

2 Mr and Mrs Trotter have just read the two brochures on pages 91 and 92 and they are not impressed:

Mrs Trotter: I can't see the point of spending a week stuck on a canal in Staffordshire. It's all very well saying you can jump off and have a quick meal at some inn or restaurant but who's got to pay for that? And if we've got to cook our own breakfasts, I'd rather be at home in my own kitchen, thank you very much.

Mr Trotter: And as for going to Florida, no thank you. If I want to get wet and wild I'll just get the garden hose out and ask Mrs Trotter to sprinkle the lawn. Who wants to see grown men walking around dressed in bear outfits? I'm sorry, but it looks like a complete waste of money to me.

Your task is to persuade Mr and Mrs Trotter to take one of the holidays – either boating in Britain or a trip to Florida.

Create a 60-second television commercial which will make them see the attraction of the holiday, and all the advantages of being away from home.

Start by making a list of the arguments they might use for not wanting to go. Use some ideas from their comments above and from your role play. Then decide how you will argue against these in your 60-second advertisement.

Use the example below to help you with setting out your script. Or use it as the start of your own commercial.

PICTURE	SOUND
	Classical Music
Trees - summer's day Camera reveals peaceful waterway	VO[1]
	Would you prefer this ....
Sudden cut to piles of washing up at kitchen sink	...to this? Or this ...
People gathered at lock, laughing as they open the gate	to this ...?
Sudden cut to ...	

1 VO = voice-over

For another example of a commercial script layout see page 101.

Taking it further

1 Once you have written your script, you could present it to the rest of the class, or write it up with a brief explanation of the decisions you made. Explain how you persuade the Trotters, to take the holiday.

2 Imagine the Trotters are persuaded by your commercial. Imagine them on the holiday and write a story or a script showing how much they enjoy it.
For more on writing in script form see page 135 in the Drama module.

Leaflet Watch

The information swamp

All day, every day we are taking in information from the world around us. Make a list of the ways in which you are swamped by information every day.

All of these sources are giving you pieces of information, even when you are not really paying attention. So if people are constantly receiving so many messages, how do advertisers make sure that their particular message reaches them?

Starting a campaign

For example, imagine you wanted to start a campaign to make more primary school children take care when crossing the road, how would you do it? Below are some possible methods. Copy out the table and discuss each method, noting down its advantages and disadvantages.

Which other methods can you think of? What are the advantages and disadvantages of each one? Add these to your table.

Method	Advantages	Disadvantages
Visiting primary schools and talking to pupils		
Using a TV commercial		
Putting up posters in the neighbourhood		
Sending a letter to all Y6 pupils		
Asking the Council to put up warning signs near all primary schools		
Giving out leaflets		

More than Meets the Eye

One very popular way of providing information to people is to design a leaflet. Look at the examples here and on page 98. One is designed chiefly to inform: it is a leaflet issued by the Body Shop to tell people about Aromatherapy.

The other is designed to persuade: it is a Government leaflet intended to persuade people to drive carefully.

However, in both of them, the purposes of informing and persuading overlap – after all, both are offering the reader information.

THE BODY SHOP
Aromatherapy

Relaxing

The quick way to unwind.

Reviving

To give your spirits a lift.

AROMATHERAPY RELAXING RANGE

Relaxing Face Mask
Unwind with this gel-based face mask containing a blend of sandalwood and lavender essential oils.

Relaxing Moisture Cream
A versatile moisturiser - for all over aromatherapy! This blend of geranium, ho wood, petitgrain and neroli essential oils will soothe and relax your face and body, and keep your skin soft and supple.

Relaxing Bath Oil
For a good night's rest, soak in this soothing blend of ylang ylang, frankincense and sandalwood essential oils.

Relaxing Warming Cream
Give tired, overworked muscles a treat with this soothing blend of bay, sweet marjoram and lavender essential oils.

Relaxing Massage Oil
Wind down after a hard day with a soothing massage using this relaxing blend of ylang ylang, vetiver and sandalwood essential oils.

BURNING OIL

Relaxing Burning Oil
A blend of relaxing and soothing essential oils to create a tranquil atmosphere in any room. Use with The Body Shop Aroma Jar.

BATH BEADS

Relaxing Bath Bead
An exotic blend of ylang ylang, bay, lavender and vetiver essential oils to soothe body and soul. Paprika gives this bead its warm orange colour.

Soothing Bath Bead
This sensuous blend of frankincense, sandalwood and patchouli is relaxing and moisturising. The soothing brown colour is a combination of paprika and chlorophyll.

ARO[M] OUT

Going [...] aroma[...] popul[...] volunt[...] count[...] clubs [...] benefit[...]

For exam[...] with elde[...] while disa[...] and foot m[...] aromather[...] community [...] develop as [...]

MASS[A]

Do [en]joy!
- use a q[...]
- make s[...]
- always [...]
- massage [...]
- make s[...] is comfor[...]
- wear loo[...] movement
- be sure y[...] your
- pour you[...] you need t[...]

Don't
- wear [...] the ma[...]
- ma[...] abd[...] vei[...] in[...]
- ar [...]ectly

[...] roblem [...] bath

RELAXING OILS

Camomile Oil
Camomile has long been used to relax babies and infants, but it's ideal for soothing dry and sensitive skin of all ages. Use in the bath, apply directly to your skin or as a compress.

Lavender Oil
A soothing and relaxing oil, especially for sensitive skin or skin which has been over-exposed to the sun. Use in the bath, massage onto your skin or inhale.

Neroli Oil
When you need to unwind, try a little of this exceptionally relaxing oil. Apply directly to your skin or add to the bath.

Rose Oil
Soften and soothe dry or mature skin with this delicate oil. Add to the bath or massage onto the skin. Ideal for a facial.

Ylang Ylang Oil
Use this exotic, relaxing oil to soften and soothe your skin. Add to a bath or massage directly onto your skin.

ALL

Single [...] tradit[...] years [...] alike [...] to a [...]

We [...] arom[...] lots o[...] effect [...] Shop'[...] in grape[...] worry a[...] to use s[...]

We've c[...] because [...] versatile [...] face, bo[...] warning[...] Aroma[...]

WARN[...] when di[...] people wi[...] selection o[...] still unsure [...] GP before [...] the first thre[...] Lavender, Ro[...] Thyme, Essen[...] Rosemary, Sa[...]

SPEED'S THE REAL KILLER

There are some drivers who think that, whatever the conditions, they can slam their foot down, go as fast as they like and still stay safe. Then, when something – or someone – gets in their way, all they have to do is hit the brake.

Get real. Speed not only burns up expensive petrol. It also means 1,000 people are killed and 77,000 injured every year. Think about it: that's the equivalent of 156 full jumbo jets. Ease off!

TEST BED

IF WE WERE ALL TO SLOW DOWN BY AN AVERAGE OF 1MPH, WE'D SAVE...

☐ 100 LIVES A YEAR?
☐ 150 LIVES A YEAR?
☐ 300 LIVES A YEAR?

WANT TO BE A LOSER?

Want to lose your licence? Or your no-claims bonus? Or even your life? In the end it's your decision.

GRAVE IMPLICATIONS

You're driving at 20mph. You hit a little girl crossing the road. There's a 1 in 20 chance you've killed her.

You've upped your speed to 30mph. Now there's a 50-50 chance she'll end up seriously dead.

At 40mph, forget it. Her chances of survival are virtually nil.

AT YOUR TIME OF LIFE, YOU SHOULD BE SLOWING DOWN A BIT

Alternatively, you could pull out and risk that suicidal overtake. But how far would it get you? Ever noticed those drivers who carve you up to get to the front of the traffic only to find out that when they've got to the next lights, everyone's caught up with them?

THE ANSWER IS 300 LIVES. And for a measly 1mph, it would be worth it. Right?

Reading in detail

1 Read both leaflets carefully. Then with a partner, discuss and make notes about:
   - the facts you learn from them
   - the devices which are used to make the layout eye-catching (pictures, logos, graphic designs, lettering)
   - the kind of language used (simple? difficult to follow? examples of jokes or word-play? chatty or formal style?)
   - who the leaflets are aimed at. How can you tell?
   - points you like about the leaflets
   - suggestions for how the leaflets could have been improved – in their use of language, design, and colour

   Give each one a star rating from 1 to 5.

2 Collect your notes together to summarize the strengths and weaknesses of each leaflet. Then share your results with the rest of the class – either on a blackboard, chart, or using an overhead projector.

Design points

If a leaflet is to be successful at persuading its readers, it needs the following ingredients:

- a firm idea about who it is aimed at – its **audience**
- clear layout
- clear use of language, which is neither too complex nor too simple

1 Look at this leaflet designed to inform young people about Shakespeare. In pairs, make a list of what you like about it and what you dislike.

2 Discuss what you think is wrong with this leaflet? What makes it so boring to read?

3 What advice would you give to the writer about:
- improving the layout
- making the language more interesting

WILLIAM SHAKESPEARE

William Shakespeare was born in Stratford-upon-Avon in 1564 and he died in 1616. He was 52 years old when he died. He was a famous playwright and wrote many plays. Altogether he wrote more than 30 plays. These include: Hamlet, Macbeth, As You Like it, King Lear and The Comedy of Errors. Some of his plays are comedies and some are not. Some are tragedies. Some are histories. His father was a glove-maker. Shakespeare married Anne Hathaway. They had three children: Susanna, Judith and Hamnet. Then Shakespeare left Stratford to go to London. He began work as an actor and then began to write his own plays. Many of his plays were performed at the Globe Theatre in London. In around 1610 Shakespeare retired to Stratford, a wealthy man, where he died.

Taking it further

1 How could you use questions and headings to improve the text? How could you write it in a more lively style? Have a go at rewriting the Shakespeare leaflet, using the information given here. Your aim is to persuade a young reader that Shakespeare's life is interesting and to encourage them to read some of his plays

2 You could instead design a leaflet for one of the following topics, aimed at persuading a young reader to find out more about:
- a certain type of music
- a famous person
- a guide to the different activities going on at your school

Use the hints below to plan your leaflet.

- Use brief paragraphs.
- Use headings to help people find their way around the leaflet.
- Have an eye-catching heading and image (picture or logo) in the top half.
- Use dark and light tones to create strong contrasts.
- Think carefully about the style of writing chosen for headings – copy the style of writing used in other leaflets and magazines.

3 Collect some leaflets from supermarkets, charities, health centres, and write about those you think work best and those that are least successful. Talk about the use of design, the language, and their appeal for the chosen audience.

Media Texts

Simply Take

In 1991 the supermarket company, Sainsbury's, began a series of 60-second television advertisements using recipes. They describe the idea like this:

'The TV celebrity recipe advertisements are designed to show viewers how to prepare and cook simple but delicious recipes using quality ingredients from Sainsbury's. The voice of the celebrity takes the viewer through the recipe with the celebrity's identity being revealed at the end of the recipe.

Not only do these advertisements display the range and quality of Sainsbury's food, but they also give a recipe idea to existing and potential customers. Recipe cards are displayed in-store for the customer to take home and keep.'

What makes it memorable?

1 Do you remember any of these commercials? Which ones stick in your memory? Why?

- Was it the recipe?
- Did you guess who the celebrity was from their voice?

2 Now watch the TV commercial just once on video and in a group of four discuss:

- why you think Philip Schofield was chosen as the celebrity for this recipe for Beef Stir Fry
- what you like/dislike about the commercial

Reading the script

What did the script for this commercial look like on the page?

1 Look at the video script on page 101 and see how well you can follow the recipe instructions without actually seeing the commercial. Does the recipe seem easy to follow? (You might find the glossary of terms at the bottom of the page useful.)

2 In pairs, practise reading the script aloud, so that your delivery sounds natural. Decide who will be A and B. A should be the performer and B the listener. After one reading, B should make suggestions about:

- when to speed up and slow down
- which words need to be pronounced more clearly
- the overall rhythm of the performance

Then try a second reading.

Video Script

SAINSBURY'S

60 seconds

'Philip Schofield' (Recording Script 3)

PICTURE

Camera follows action throughout. Close-ups of food against a dark background.

SOUND
(Music under)
<u>Philip VO:</u>
Cut 12 oz of Sainsbury's steak into strips

Now take a tablespoon of cornflour...

a little Sainsbury's Chinese 5 spice...

and 3 tablespoons of soy sauce.

Mix and marinate the meat for 20 minutes.

Meanwhile finely chop one clove of garlic...
a little ginger...
and 6 oz of broccoli.

Next, slice some salad onions, a red pepper...
and you're ready to cook.

Heat 2 tablespoons of Sainsbury's sesame oil in a wok.

Add marinated steak; garlic and ginger, and fry for 3 minutes.

Pop in the broccoli, the peppers, and onions, and cook for another 2 minutes.

Now add a splash of sherry and a little water...

With the lid on, steam for a minute - then serve with Sainsbury's Thai fragrant rice.

Chopsticks are optional.

PICTURE
We cut to see finished dish.
Chopsticks lift piece of meat out of frame. We follow to see Philip Schofield. He smiles at camera.

MVO: Sainsbury's. Everyone's favourite ingredient.

We dissolve to super:
Sainsbury's. Everyone's favourite ingredient.

Glossary

1 **VO** = voice over
2 **MVO** = male voice over
3 **cut** = a quick change to a different image
4 **dissolve** = a slow fade to a different image
5 **super** = words placed over the top of the main image (superimposed)

Vision only

Now watch the commercial again, this time with the sound turned down. As you watch, concentrate on the way the food is presented; how one image changes to another; and how Philip Schofield is presented at the end. In particular, make notes on the following:

■ how is the food made to look attractive
■ what effect the dark background has
■ what effect having no sound has on your impression of the commercial
■ how is Philip Schofield dressed? What is his expression?

Sound only

When you have discussed your ideas as a class, play the video again. This time black out the screen and listen to the soundtrack only. Make notes about:

■ the kind of music that is used. What does it sound like or make you think of? Why do you think the music was chosen?
■ Would you have guessed that this was Philip Schofield's voice? Try to describe the kind of voice he has.
■ How does he read the script? Can you tell that he is reading? Does he read slowly, quickly? Where does he vary the pace?

Final viewing

1 Now watch the commercial for a final time, paying attention to both vision and sound. Decide:
   - who you think it is aimed at
   - how successful the commercial is
   - whether it would make you try the recipe and/or shop more at Sainsbury's

2 Finally, why do you think Philip Schofield was chosen to appear in the commercial? The comments below from Jonny Sherwin at the advertising agency Abbot Mead Vickers BBDO should aid your discussion.

Why Philip Schofield?

'At the time, he was becoming exceptionally popular, not just as a main presenter of BBC's *Going Live* but also in his new role in Joseph the musical – i.e. a stage star as well as a TV star.

He was also the ideal person to bring some popular youth appeal to the campaign whilst being popular with the broader age-range of our target audience (he was especially popular with mums).

He has an interest in cooking; the contemporary nature suits his personality.

He was also an advertising newcomer at the time.'

Jonny Sherwin

Recipe Cards

Sainsbury's also produced a free recipe card to go alongside the TV commercial.

As seen on TV

SAINSBURY'S
Recipe for
Beef Stir Fry

**Sainsbury's.
Everyone's favourite
ingredient.**

Simply take ...

- 375g (12oz) rump, sirloin or fillet steak, cut into very thin strips
- 1½ level tablespoons cornflour
- ¼ teaspoon Chinese 5-spice
- 3 tablespoons light or dark soy sauce
- 175g (6oz) broccoli
- 2 tablespoons sesame oil
- 1 tablespoon chopped, fresh ginger
- 1 clove garlic, finely chopped
- 1 red pepper, thinly sliced
- 1 bunch salad onions, sliced diagonally
- 4-5 tablespoons sherry
- 2 tablespoons water
- serve with Thai fragrant rice

1. Place the steak in a bowl with the cornflour, Chinese 5-spice and soy sauce. Mix well and leave to marinate for 20 minutes.
2. Meanwhile, split the broccoli into florets. Slice the stalks diagonally into thin oval shapes and the florets into small heads.
3. Heat the oil in a wok or large frying pan, add the marinated steak, ginger and garlic and stir fry for 3 or 4 minutes.
4. Add the pepper, broccoli, and the salad onions and stir fry for 2 minutes.
5. Add the sherry and water, put a lid on the pan and steam for 1 minute. Transfer to a warmed serving dish and serve immediately with the rice.

Cooking time: Approximately 10 minutes
Serves: 4

There are lots of delicious alternative ingredients for this recipe:
- Use thin strips of chicken or pork fillet in place of beef.
- Alternative vegetables such as beansprouts, mange tout, mushrooms and onions can be substituted.
- Use olive or groundnut oil instead of sesame oil.
- Use 4-5 tablespoons of beef stock in place of sherry.
- Garlic granules can be used instead of fresh garlic.
- Add a few cashew nuts, watercbestnuts or canned bamboo shoots for extra crunch.
- Delicious served with egg noodles.
- Sprinkle with sesame seeds to garnish.
- Use ground ginger instead of fresh.

Wine suggestion: Sainsbury's Vin de Pays des Côteaux des Baronnies Gamay 75cl.

All products subject to availability. Some products available in larger stores only.

**Sainsbury's.
Everyone's favourite ingredient.**

729/293

What makes the difference?

1 Compare the recipe instructions on the card with the ones in the video script on page 101. Make notes about any differences you notice. Which has more information? How do the words differ? How can you tell that one is designed to be spoken aloud and the other to be read?
  What do you like about the layout? How would you change the overall design?

2 It would be easy to think that the Sainsbury's 'Simply Take' campaign was designed purely to inform people about a recipe. But of course it is also designed to persuade. Discuss what you think it tries to persuade customers to think and to do.

Taking it further

1 Choose your own favourite recipe, or make one up. Then design a 60-second TV commercial for an audience of your age.
  ■ Choose your celebrity and write about why you have selected her or him.
  ■ Write the script, using the same style as the Sainsbury's commercial. Remember to include ideas for some background music.
  ■ Practise performing the script, miming the stages in the recipe.

2 You might also design a recipe card to accompany your commercial. Think carefully about how your instructions will differ from the TV commercial script.
  Look at this example, designed by a student using a desk-top publishing package. What do you notice about:
  ■ the language he has used for the instructions
  ■ the way he has used layout
  ■ the type/graphics used in headings

Pasta Alla Polpettine

Delicious balls of savoury mince with onion and garlic, served in a rich tomato and mushroom sauce with pasta.

Simply take ...
700g best quality minced beef
2 tbsp grated onion
2 cloves garlic, peeled and crushed
1 tbsp chopped parsley
salt and freshly ground black pepper
For the sauce:
1 onion, peeled and finely chopped
2 cloves garlic peeled and crushed
100g button mushrooms
400g can chopped tomatoes
1 tbsp tomato puree
half a wineglass of red wine

Mix mince with onion, garlic and parsley in a bowl. Season and mix well with hands. Nip off chunks of mince mix and form into walnut-sized balls by rolling between palms of hands. Reserve in the fridge. For the sauce, heat 2 tbsp oil in a pan and fry onion, garlic and mushrooms until soft but not browned. Stir in tomatoes, tomato puree and wine and bring to bubbling. Simmer until slightly reduced and thickened. Season. Remove from heat. Heat 2 tbsp oil and fry meat balls until browned all over and almost cooked. Pour over sauce and check seasoning. Bubble for another 3 minutes until the balls are completely cooked. Serve with freshly cooked spaghetti.

NEW

Andy's
Recipe For
Pasta Alla Polpettine

Autobiography
Turning Points

What has been the most important point in your life so far – the minute, hour, day or week which made the strongest and most lasting impression on you? Look at this list made by a group of Year 7 students:

> Moving house
> A pet dying
> Changing schools
> Winning in sport
> Getting into serious trouble

In pairs or groups of four, discuss the kind of events which stick in your minds. Are they:

- usually happy
- usually unhappy
- from the recent past
- from the distant past
- personal,
- connected with family, or with friends?

Looking at the motive

In **autobiography**, a person writes about the stories of his or her life. You can see this in the original Greek meanings of the word: auto + bio + graphy

> auto = 'self'
> bio = 'life'
> graphy = 'writing'

So an autobiography is 'self-life-writing' – a piece of writing about your own life. Why do you think people write autobiographies? In your pair or small groups, discuss these different possibilities:

- to make money
- to tell people about important events that have happened to them
- because people like to read about famous people
- to sort out the events in their own lives
- because autobiography is enjoyable to write
- because they are big-headed

Which ideas do you agree with and which do you disagree with? Which idea do you most agree with? Can you think of other reasons?

Strong Impressions

On pages 107–109 are three extracts in which writers describe events which have made a strong impression upon them. Bethany Veney was a slave in Virginia, USA, until 1858. Here she recalls her first memory.

The Narrative of Bethany Veney

I have little recollection of my very early life. My mother and her five children were owned by one James Fletcher, Pass Run, town of Luray, Page County, Virginia. Of my father I know nothing.

The first thing I remember with any distinctness was when, about seven years old, I was, with other children, knocking apples from a tree, when we were surprised by my young mistress, Miss Nasenath Fletcher, calling to us, in a loud and threatening tone, demanding what we were doing. Without waiting for a reply, she told us to follow her; and, as she led the way down to a blackberry pasture not far off, she endeavoured, in a very solemn manner, to impress us with the importance of always telling the truth. 'If asked a question,' she said, 'we must answer directly, yes or no.' I asked her, 'What we must say if asked something which we did not know.' She answered, 'Why, you must say you don't know, of course.' I said, 'I shall say, "Maybe 'tis, and maybe 'tain't".' I remember well how the children laughed at this; and then Miss Nasenath went on to tell us that some time all this world that we saw would be burned up, – that the moon would be turned into blood, the stars would fall out of the sky, and everything would melt away with a great heat, and that everybody, every little child that had told a lie, would be cast into a lake of fire and brimstone, and would burn there for ever and ever, and, what was more, though they should burn for ever and ever, they would never be burned up.

I was dreadfully frightened; and, as soon as I could get away, I ran to my mammy, and, repeating what mistress had said, begged to know if it could be true. To my great sorrow, she confirmed it all, but added what Miss Nasenath had failed to do; namely, that those who told the truth and were good would always have everything they should want. It seemed to me then there was nothing so good as molasses and sugar; and I eagerly asked, 'Shall I have all the molasses and sugar I want, if I tell the truth?' 'Yes,' she replied, 'If you are good; but remember, if you tell lies, you will be burned in the lake that burns for ever and ever.'

This made a very strong impression upon me. I can never forget my mammy's manner at the time. I believed every word she said, and from that day to this I have never doubted its truth.

Bethany Veney

Michael Buerk is a journalist and newsreader for BBC News. In the Ethiopian famine of 1984 his reports of the suffering there shocked the world and led to the Live Aid charity appeal. Here he remembers one moment from the experience:

I'll Never Forget the Day

I'll never forget the day that I found out what desperate hunger is really like for so many millions of people, who live on the very borders of existence.

My camera team and I had been filming the results of the Ethiopian famine. We had spent several days watching people die in front of us, children as well as adults, and seen tens of thousands of poor Ethiopians who did not seem far away from that fate. We were, I realize now, in a mild state of shock. So much horror around; such an enormous scale of suffering.

It was a paradox of this famine that when we went into a village in the middle of the worst affected area we found a café of sorts that was not only open but sold Coca-Cola and bread rolls. We sat in the corner of this mud room and were about to have these things for breakfast when there was a commotion at the door.

There must have been several hundred starving people fighting for a chance to see somebody eating.

At the very front was an old man, lined and wiry. His eyes were wide and his hands were trembling. He fell to his knees and, very slowly, started to move towards us across the floor with both hands stretched out, begging, in front of him.

Who could have eaten under those circumstances? But what could we do? We gave the old man some bread and went out into the street and, in a pathetic sort of way, tried to break up the rolls to feed all those people.

I have never felt so useless and I'm sure my colleagues felt the same. There was really nothing any of us could say to each other for some time after.

Michael Buerk

The well known writer, Laurie Lee, here describes a very early memory of his from the First World War.

The Golden Cross

I'll never forget the day – was it my earliest memory? – when I crawled up the steps into the back garden of the Slad Road house where I was born. The first war was on. I must have been about two-and-a-half years old. I was sitting on a stone in the garden, looking down over Stroud, when suddenly a great golden cross rose in the sky above the fence, hovered still for a moment, then plunged back down again.

The cross was radiant, dazzling, but I didn't mention it to my family, imagining that golden crosses in the sky were a normal part of the world. Later I heard that an airplane had crashed near Stroud at that time, somewhere on one of the hills. I didn't know what an airplane was, but I had seen one from my perch in the garden, and it has crashed in the light of the setting sun.

Laurie Lee

What makes it real?

1 In a group of three discuss how you can tell that these three extracts are auto-biographical rather than excerpts from novels? Pick out one or two sentences from each one which show that it is real.

2 One feature of the extracts is that they are written in the **first person**. That means they say 'I' and 'me', rather than 'he', 'she' or 'they' (which is called the **third person**).
How does writing in the first person make the memories come to life? Find out by rewriting the first two paragraphs of Michael Buerk's extract in the third person (he/she/they). The first sentence is done for you.

> Michael Buerk will never forget the day that he found out what desperate hunger is really like…

3 What has been lost from the extract in the rewriting?

Taking it further

1 Choose an important moment from your life and write about it in the first person. To bring the event to life, remember to:
■ give background details – who is involved, where and when
■ if other people were involved, describe them – their appearance, speech, behaviour
■ use dialogue to show what people said
■ describe your feelings and how the event has changed you
Your starting-point might be:
> 'I'll never forget the day when …'

2 Interview a parent or grandparent about a key moment in their lives. Try to find out what it was like to be there, exactly what happened, who they were with. You could record your interview. Then write the account up in the third person. Your opening sentence might read something like this:
> 'A key moment in my grandfather's life was when he…'

Language Study
Different Dialects

What is a dialect?

In her account of her childhood, on page 107, Bethany Veney gives the exact words that she would use if she did not know the answer to a question. She tells her mistress that she would reply:

'Maybe 'tis, and maybe 'tain't.'

The phrase she uses is part of her day-to-day dialect. What would you have replied in your local dialect? Would you have said 'perhaps' rather than 'maybe'? Or 'it isn't' or 'it's not' rather than ''tain't'?

A **dialect** is a variety of language used by a particular group of people (usually, but not always, from the same region). It has its own words and expressions and its own grammatical rules.

Standard English dialect

Everything that we say or write is in a dialect. The sentence that you are reading at this moment is itself in a dialect, but one which is special in a number of ways:

■ it can be spoken or written in any part of the English-speaking world
■ it does not 'belong' to any single group of people

Because it is a dialect that is used in nearly all written English, and is therefore the one that everybody understands, it is called **Standard English dialect**.

Standard English everywhere

We meet Standard English every time we read a newspaper, open a magazine or pick up an advertising leaflet.

All of the cuttings on this page come from extracts in this book. They are all in Standard English.

Try to identify where each one comes from and then write down the type of writing it is (e.g. newspaper article, autobiography, advertisement...). Set out your answers in a chart like this:

Some Uses of Standard English

Cutting	From page...	Type of writing
A	91	Travel brochure

A

The watery possibilities here are endless.

B

Transfer to a warmed serving dish and serve immediately with the rice

C

As the old woman came near she heard drumming and singing.

D

I still hear other children calling you 'Tyke'.

E

'Black arrow! I have saved you to the last.'

F

They had called him... the Warlord.

H

Remove the inner tube then inflate it.

G

Apply directly to your skin or add to the bath.

I

It has high, arched windows through which can be seen mountains and forest.

J

His eyes were wide and his hands were trembling.

Paragraphs

A **paragraph** is a block of sentences in writing. The sentences in a paragraph will usually be linked together by one overall idea or topic. For example, in the leaflet 'Entertainment Florida Style' on page 92, the topic headings for each paragraph have been written in. In this case, each one is the name of the attraction being described in that paragraph.

Paragraphs in the best order

1 Instructions

On page 83 you were asked to place the six paragraphs about cleaning your teeth in the right order.

One way to do this might be to take each paragraph and give it a topic heading. Using the jumbled order printed on page 83, we might say that the topic headings were:

1 Cleaning the gums
2 When to clean and for how long
3 Choosing a good toothbrush
4 Repeat the process
5 Using the toothpaste
6 Rinsing
7 Method of brushing teeth

These headings should help you to decide that the logical order is: 3, 5, 7, 1, 4, 6, 2.

Here is another activity to help you see how paragraphs work in a set of written instructions.

1 Working in pairs, one person takes the instructions for repairing a puncture on page 82 and the other person the recipe on page 104.

2 Copy out your set of instructions on to a sheet of paper, cut them up into paragraphs and rearrange them into a new order. (If you have access to a word-processor, type them in and use the cut-and-paste facility to change the order.)

3 Swap your sets of instructions.

4 Look at the paragraphs you have received and give each one a topic heading.

5 Put them in the right order.

6 Finally, check your versions with the original ones.

2 Stories

For a set of instructions, there is usually a 'right' order, which can be tested out: either the instructions work in a particular order, or they do not!

It can be much harder to decide where paragraphs should go in a story, where there is no such 'right' order.

On page 40 you were asked to punctuate a creation myth by Ted Hughes: *Why The Owl Behaves As He Does*. Now make it clearer still dividing it into paragraphs. You have been given a suggested topic heading for each paragraph as well as the approximate length. (To make the task more interesting, the topic headings are not in the right order!)

Owl myth topic headings:

Owl puts plan into practice	(8 lines)
It is the same to this day	(4 lines)
Birds discover what is going on	(2 lines)
Owl's plan	(2 lines)
The birds sing in the trees	(1 line)
The birds mob Owl	(4 lines)

3 Information

The article about Diving on page 87 shows how paragraphs are used in a piece of writing which is giving information.

Look at the section in the article from 'Divers may go beneath the surface…' to '…it will kill them.' The information is divided into five paragraphs.

Give each one a topic heading and then compare yours with the suggestions which your teacher will give you.

Writing from topic headings

Here are three sets of paragraph topic headings (in the right order!). The first is for a set of instructions on how to use a coin telephone; the second for a well known story; the third for information about butterflies.

Choose either A, B, or C and write the paragraphs to create the complete text, using the topic headings as guides.

To write full and interesting pieces, you might need to do some further research. This might include consulting other people, books, or a CD-Rom. For more on using CD-Rom see page 89.

How to use a public (coin) telephone
(Make this clear for a visitor to this country.)

Lifting the receiver and inserting the money
Dialling
Checking how your money is being used up
Making a follow-on call
Collecting unused money

The story of the Pied Piper
(Write this for someone who does not know the story at all.)

Hamelin is plagued with rats
The desperate people threaten the Mayor
The Piper arrives and makes an offer
How the Piper gets rid of the rats
The Mayor goes back on his bargain
The Piper's revenge

Information about butterflies
(Assume that you are writing for a child who does not know very much about the subject.)

Butterfly lays eggs on the right leaves
Caterpillar hatches from each egg
Caterpillar feeds
Forms a chrysalis
Butterfly emerges

About Sentences

Three types of sentence

On page 99 of the Non-fiction module, you were asked why the leaflet on Shakespeare was so boring. One reason was that there was not much variety in the kinds of sentence used.

Simple sentences

Most of them were what we call simple sentences. A **simple sentence** is one that says only one thing:

> e.g. He was a famous playwright.
>   He wrote many great plays.

Coordinated sentences

The Shakespeare article also contains a few coordinated sentences. A **coordinated sentence** is what you get when you join two simple sentences together with 'or', 'and', or 'but'.

> e.g. He was a famous playwright *and* he wrote many great plays.

Complex sentences

If you use a word which actually shows how the two parts of the sentence are joined in meaning, you get a **complex sentence**.

> e.g. He was a famous playwright *because* he wrote many great plays.

If a piece of writing contains too many examples of the same kind of sentence, as the Shakespeare leaflet does, it can become rather dull and flat.

Complex sentences and conjunctions

The example of a complex sentence above is more interesting and more useful, because it gives the reason *why* Shakespeare became famous ('...because he wrote many great plays.').

The word that joins the two parts of a coordinated or complex sentence together (e.g. 'and' or 'because') is called a **conjunction**.

1 Here are two columns of simple sentences and, beneath them, a list of common conjunctions.

Join each pair of simple sentences, to make a complex sentence, using a conjunction which will show how the two are connected in meaning. For example, the first pair might become:

> The Egyptians believed aromatic oils were so effective *because* they had been formulated by the gods.

Write out your answers and then compare them with a partner's.

Column 1	Column 2	
The Egyptians believed aromatic oils were so effective	they had been formulated by the gods.	
This man is Pyramus	you would know.	(141)
I'm angry	the people love you..	(10)
We would make him our king	we could get him to wear a crown.	(16)
The man in the shop did show me	I can't quite remember.	(24)
He rooted among them	he found a little book.	(19)
He couldn't blow it down	it was stuck to the ground.	(22)

Some conjunctions

because   if   but   as   when   though   until   while   unless   before   since

2 Very often, the conjunction which joins the two simple sentences comes at the beginning of the new sentence, rather than in between the two simple sentences.

Join up the following pairs of sentences, this time placing the conjunction at the beginning. For example, the first pair might become:

> *As* the old woman came near, she heard drumming and singing.

Column 1	Column 2	
the old woman came near	she heard drumming and singing.	(12)
the people began to shrink	Nokomis spoke.	(13)
the rain stopped	the water drained away.	(13)
he is huge and strong	he is very quiet.	(16)
that had astonished Keill	he was astonished even more by the story.	(26)

The numbers in brackets refer to the page on which the original complex sentence can be found. Check to see whether or not you chose the same conjunction.

Adjectives

Look back at Michael Buerk's account of his experience in Ethiopia on page 108. To describe to us what the situation was really like, and how he felt about it, he employs a number of extremely important and effective words.

In setting the scene he writes:

> I'll never forget the day that I found out what *desperate* hunger is really like... such an *enormous* scale of suffering...

Describing the starving people he writes:

> At the very front was an *old* man, *lined* and *wiry*. His eyes were *wide*...

And, to make us understand his own feelings he writes:

> I have never felt so *useless*.

All of these highlighted words are **adjectives**. Adjectives are powerful words, as you can see, because they help to describe a person, place, thing, or feeling. In other words they add information to a noun or pronoun. (A **pronoun** is a word that takes the place of a noun, such as I, you, he, she, it, they, we.)

Adjective	Noun	or	Pronoun
desperate	hunger		
enormous	scale		
old lined wiry	man		
wide	eyes		
useless			I

Adjectives for persuasion

In the Hoseasons travel brochure on page 91, adjectives play an important part in persuading the reader that a boating holiday is just the thing they need.

1   Turn back to page 91 and find the following nouns (and one pronoun) in the opening paragraphs (down as far as '...historic towns.'). Then write down the adjectives that go with them:

> choice, time, It, world, atmosphere, attractions, freedom, aspects, areas, waterways, pace, towns

2   Most of the nouns are words that you would expect to find in a piece of writing about a holiday: choice, time, attractions. What did you notice about the collection of adjectives? What was there that linked them?

3   Look at the final section (from 'You'll also meet...').
    Find four adjectives to describe people:
    ■ two that describe the holiday-makers
    ■ one that describes the boat-yard staff
    ■ one that describes you on holiday.
    Find three adjectives to describe places.

Taking it further

The extracts which follow are from the column headed 'Aromatherapy Relaxing Range' from the Body Shop leaflet in this module.

Read them carefully in pairs. Try to remember or work out which adjectives would go with the highlighted nouns, using the list given below.

Then look back at page 97 to compare your ideas with the original.

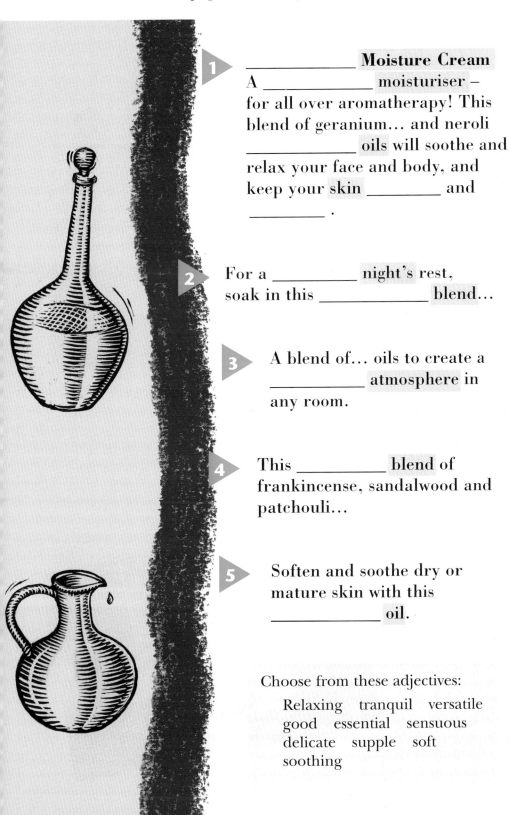

1 _____ **Moisture Cream**

A _____ moisturiser – for all over aromatherapy! This blend of geranium... and neroli _____ oils will soothe and relax your face and body, and keep your skin _____ and _____ .

2 For a _____ night's rest, soak in this _____ blend...

3 A blend of... oils to create a _____ atmosphere in any room.

4 This _____ blend of frankincense, sandalwood and patchouli...

5 Soften and soothe dry or mature skin with this _____ oil.

Choose from these adjectives:

Relaxing   tranquil   versatile
good   essential   sensuous
delicate   supple   soft
soothing

Inventing and Performing
Inventing a Story

Stages in creating a scene

In groups of five, choose one of the situations from these cartoons and use it as the starting point for a three-minute play scene.

You are not trying to create a whole play and therefore do not have to bring your scene to a proper conclusion. You are simply going to act out what happens next.

Preparing the scene

1 First of all, decide what is happening in the picture.

Think about:
- the actions (What actually has happened? How did it happen?)
- the characters (Who are the people in the scene? What are they like? How might they behave in a situation like this?)
- the setting (Where is it taking place?)

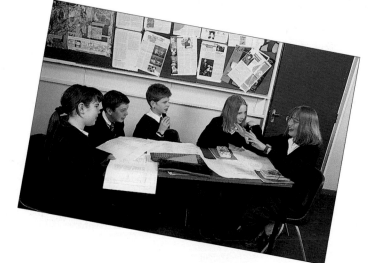

2 Discuss possible things that might happen next, remembering your group's suggestions about what has happened already and how the characters are likely to behave.

3 After you have discussed several possibilities for what might happen next, select one to act out.
- Choose events which are likely to interest an audience and which are possible to act out in the next few minutes in the classroom.
- Think very carefully about the characters in your story and the ways in which they might behave.

4 Next decide who is going to take which part, making sure that you give everyone in the group something interesting to do.

Acting it out

5 When you are ready, act out the scene, using only the small space around you. Do not prepare any speeches beforehand, but simply say words as they come to you, just as your character would in a real situation. This is known as **improvising**.

6 When you have come to the end of your improvisation, discuss:
- which parts were particularly successful
- which ones might need to be changed

7 Then act out the scene again, trying to improve upon your first version.

Performing and watching

8 When you are ready, perform your scene for the rest of the class. Make a tape-recording of your scene so that you can look back at your performance.

9 You will also be able to watch other groups' performances and discuss them. In what ways were their scenes different from your group's?
- Which parts did you enjoy most?
- Were there any ideas which you might 'borrow' for use in future improvisations?

Building Characters

Understanding a script

Scenes that you improvise in class often work best when the characters seem real and interesting.

Read this extract in pairs and notice how everything the characters say helps us to build up a picture of the kind of people they are.

It comes from a play written by Gene Kemp, based on her novel, *The Turbulent Term of Tyke Tyler*. The scene takes place in a school corridor.

Tyke Tyler

Mrs Somers: What are you doing here?

Tyke: Taking tea money.

Mrs Somers: Don't mumble, child. And look up when a member of staff speaks to you.

Tyke: Yes, Miss.

Mrs Somers: And another thing. I still hear other children calling you 'Tyke'. You have a perfectly good name, haven't you?

Tyke: Yes, Miss.

Mrs Somers: You haven't forgotten it, have you?

Tyke: No, Miss.

Mrs Somers: Well, use it. Now run along.

(**Mrs Somers** *sweeps off.* **Tyke** *makes a monster face after her. As* **Mrs Somers** *turns back,* **Tyke** *tries to wipe the face off quickly.*)

Mrs Somers: Well, move!

(Act 1 Scene 1)

Gene Kemp

Looking at the dialogue

The words that characters speak in a play are known as the **dialogue**. How much can you tell about these characters and the way they might be acted, from their words in this short scene?

1 What kind of person is Mrs Somers?
- Is she a popular teacher? Is she usually good-tempered? How can you tell?
- How should she speak in this scene? (Slowly? Snappily? Calmly?)
- What does she think about Tyke?

2 What about Tyke?
- Is Tyke popular with classmates?
- How does Tyke reply when Mrs Somers asks 'What are you doing here?' (Boldly? Shyly? Confidently?) How do we know?
- What is Tyke's opinion of Mrs Somers?

3 Now that you have discussed the two characters, act out the scene again. Try to use your new knowledge about them and the way they are behaving, to make them sound realistic and interesting.

4 When you have done that, compare your version with the one on the video. Did you make the same decisions as the actors about how the characters ought to behave?

Improvising as a character

In pairs, read the following descriptions of two characters. Then use what you know to improvise a short conversation between them, to last about half a minute. Make sure that the things your characters say show what kinds of people they are.

Imagine that it is Monday morning and Brown has just opened the front door to find Simkins on the step...

Name: Derek Brown.

Occupation:
House-cleaner.

Character:
Gloomy; hates people who waffle; bad-tempered. At the moment, really fed up, because his 'Kleen-U-Up' vacuum cleaner has just broken down again. It needs a spare part.

Name: Eddie Simpkins

Occupation:
Door-to-door salesperson, selling 'Kleen-U-Up' vacuum cleaners and spare parts.

Character:
Cheerful; loves to tell jokes; never down-hearted. At the moment, very keen to make his first sale of the week.

Overheard on the bus

Have you ever overheard different (sometimes fascinating) snatches of conversation while on a bus or train journey? You can create your own impression of a noisy but absorbing journey in this next improvisation.

1 Each person writes down a description of a character (like the ones above). The descriptions are then collected in and given out at random to other people in the class.

2 In pairs, you then improvise short conversations between these new characters. This time, they are sitting next to each other on a journey.

3 One extra person then walks slowly past each pair. As the 'passenger' passes your seats raise the volume of your conversation. Then become quieter as they pass by. The effect is like a spoken Mexican Wave.

Focusing on Story and Character

Bringing the two together

Earlier in this unit you practised:

- improvising a **story**, based on a situation
- building up **characters**, making them say things which show what kinds of people they are

In groups of six, read this extract from Shakespeare's *A Midsummer Night's Dream*, which shows a group of characters doing very much what you yourselves have been doing: getting a play together.

As you read, think about those two elements of story and character.

A Midsummer Night's Dream

Act 1 Scene 2

(*Enter* **Quince**, **Snug**, **Bottom**, **Flute**, **Snout**, and **Starveling**.)

Quince: Is all our company here?

Bottom: You were best to call them generally, man by man, according to the scrip.

Quince: Here is the scroll of every man's name, which is thought fit, through all Athens, to play in our interlude before the duke and the duchess on his wedding-day at night.

Bottom: First, good Peter Quince, say what the play treats on; then read the names of the actors, and so grow to a point.

Quince: Marry, our play is, *The most lamentable comedy, and most cruel death of*
10 *Pyramus and Thisbe.*

Bottom: A very good piece of work, I assure you, and a merry. Now, good Peter Quince, call forth your actors by the scroll. Masters, spread yourselves.

Quince: Answer as I call you. Nick Bottom, the weaver?

Bottom: Ready! Name what part I am for, and proceed.

Quince: You, Nick Bottom, are set down for Pyramus.

Bottom: What is Pyramus? A lover, or a tyrant?

Quince: A lover, that kills himself most gallant for love.

Bottom: That will ask some tears in the true performance of it: if I do it;
20 let the audience look to their eyes! I will move storms; I will condole in some measure. To the rest – yet my chief humour is for a tyrant. I could play Ercles rarely, or a part to tear a cat in, to make all split.
The raging rocks
And shivering shocks
Shall break the locks
Of prison gates:
And make and mar
The foolish Fates.

This was lofty! Now name the rest of the players. This is Ercles' vein, a
30   tyrant's vein; a lover is more condoling.

Quince: Francis Flute, the bellows-mender?

Flute: Here, Peter Quince.

Quince: Flute, you must take Thisbe on you.

Flute: What is Thisbe? A wandering knight?

Quince: It is the lady that Pyramus must love.

Flute: Nay, faith, let me not play a woman; I have a beard coming.

Quince: That's all one: you shall play it in a mask, and you may speak as
    small as you will.

Bottom: An I may hide my face, let me play Thisbe too. I'll speak in a
40   monstrous little voice 'Thisne, Thisne!' 'Ah, Pyramus, my lover dear;
    thy Thisbe dear, and lady dear!'

Quince: No, no; you must play Pyramus; and Flute, you Thisbe.

Bottom: Well, proceed.

Quince: Robin Starveling, the tailor.

Starveling: Here, Peter Quince.

Quince: Robin Starveling, you must play Thisbe's mother. Tom Snout, the
    tinker.

Snout: Here, Peter Quince.

Quince: You, Pyramus' father; myself, Thisbe's father; Snug the joiner, you
50   the lion's part: and, I hope, here is a play fitted.

Snug: Have you the lion's part written? Pray you, if it be, give it me, for I
    am slow of study.

Quince: You may do it extempore, for it is nothing but roaring.

123

Bottom: Let me play the lion too. I will roar, that I will do any man's heart good to hear me; I will roar, that I will make the duke say, 'Let him roar again, let him roar again.'

Quince: An you should do it too terribly, you would fright the duchess and the ladies, that they would shriek; and that were enough to hang us all.

All: That would hang us, every mother's son.

60 **Bottom:** I grant you, friends, if you should fright the ladies out of their wits, they would have no more discretion but to hang us; but I will aggravate my voice so that I will roar you as gently as any suckling dove; I will roar you and 'twere any nightingale.

Quince: You can play no part but Pyramus; for Pyramus is a sweet-faced man; a proper man, as one shall see in a summer's day; a most lovely, gentleman-like man; therefore, you must needs play Pyramus.

Bottom: Well, I will undertake it. What beard were I best to play it in?

Quince: Why, what you will.

Bottom: I will discharge it in either you straw-colour beard, your orange-
70   tawny beard, your purple-in-grain beard, or your French-crown-colour beard, your perfect yellow.

Quince: Some of your French crowns have no hair at all, and then you will play bare-faced. But masters, here are your parts; and I am to entreat you, request you, and desire you, to con them by tomorrow night, and meet me in the palace wood, a mile without the town, by moonlight. There will we rehearse; for if we meet in the city, we shall be dogged with company, and our devices known. In the meantime I will draw a bill of properties, such as our play wants. I pray you, fail me not.

Bottom: We will meet; and there we may rehearse most obscenely and
80   courageously. Take pains; be perfect; adieu.

Quince: At the duke's oak we meet.

Bottom: Enough; hold, or cut bow-strings.

(Act 1 Scene 2 Lines 1–82)

William Shakespeare

Talking about the story

Peter Quince and his friends have planned to meet the next night in the Palace Wood, about a mile from the town. There, by moonlight, they will be able to rehearse in secret.

What kinds of things do you think might happen when they arrive there? (You will find out on pages 131–133.)

Talking about the characters

1 Still in your groups of six, discuss what the dialogue reveals about the characters. What kinds of people are they?

2 Split into two groups of three, one taking Peter Quince; and the other Nick Bottom. Then discuss what you know about each one from what he says in this scene. Turn back to page 121 and use the descriptions of Brown and Simpkins as a guide to writing a character profile For example: You could look particularly at these lines, when discussing these two characters.

Peter Quince:
lines: 37–38; 49–50;
64–66; 73–75

Nick Bottom:
lines: 7–8 (and 11–13);
19–30; 39–41
(and 54–56)

3 What about Flute, Snug, Starveling, and Snout?
We do not learn much about the last two in this scene, but see how much of a character profile you can draw up for Snug and Flute.

4 Choose one of the six characters and draw what *you* think he looks like and how he might be dressed.
When you have completed your profiles and illustrations, compare them with other groups' versions, to see how different they were. Although you have been reading and discussing the same scene, it is amazing how differently people can imagine what characters in a play are like.

Improvising the scene

Read the scene once more, and jot down in note form the main things that happen.

When you are sure that you are familiar with the 'framework' of the scene, close your books and improvise it, with each person in the group taking one character.
Use these guidelines:

- **The language** Do not try to repeat the exact words of the script. Use language that you would use if you were that person today, meeting up with a group of workmates to put a play together.

- **The characters** But do try to keep the characters of Quince and Bottom and the others as described in your profiles. Use everything you have learnt about the characters to bring them alive.

- **The humour** In particular, look at the most humorous moments (the way Bottom wants to play every part, for example, or Flute's unwillingness to play a woman) and try to make them as funny for an audience as possible.

In other words, use Shakespeare's characters and story, but make it part of your world.

Reading and Performing
Reading a Script

A script is nothing more than words on a page. Readers – and actors –
have to put in a lot of work in order to turn a script into a performed
play, as you will see.

A first reading

Read the following script in groups of three. This extract comes from
Guy's Thoughts, a short play by Peter Cansell.

Guy's Thoughts

Author's note: This play has three characters – two children (I have called
them Jo and Sam but their names do not matter) and Guy Fawkes.

Part 1 Scene 1

(A Garden Shed.)

Jo: (*Coming in*) Look Sam, I've got some of my dad's old trousers.
Ain't he fat!

Sam: Yeah. They'll look great with this jumper though. My mum threw
it out, said it was too worn to wear.

Jo: Who'd wear that colour anyway?

Sam: I think it's quite attractive actually. I might even keep it for myself.

Jo: Oh come on, don't do that, we won't have anything to make the
body with.

Sam: You could get something.

Jo: I've brought these trousers already, and the mask, and this hat.
You've only brought the jumper so far, and now you're taking it
away again.

Sam: No I'm not.

Jo: Yes, you are!

Sam: Not!

Jo: Well let's have it then, and we can get started.

> (*They begin stuffing the guy, and continue for the rest of the scene.*)

Sam: Jo, where are we going with it?

Jo: I've got it all worked out. We'll go down the shopping precinct
for the morning. Come home for an early dinner about 11 o'clock,
then back to the row of shops in Fish Street, before going down the
station about 5 o'clock for the commuters.

Sam: You're brilliant, you are, like an army general the way you plan
things.

Jo: Then tonight, we'll get the bonfire built, and that'll be it. It'll
all go up in smoke.

Sam: Shame, innit?

Jo: What?

Sam: All that work, just to see it all go up in smoke.

Jo: That's what Bonfire Night's all about though isn't it?

Sam: Yeah, I suppose it is.

Jo: Come on then let's finish, so we can get on with the business.

Scene 2

(A Street.)

Jo: Penny for the Guy!
Penny for the Guy!
Thank you Missus.

Sam: Why do we have to say that?

Jo: What?

Sam: Penny for the Guy.

Jo: 'Cos it's what you have to say.

Sam: But it don't make sense, does it? We don't want anyone to give us a flippin' penny, do we?

Jo: No... But it's tradition isn't it, and anyway the way you say it nobody gives us anything. You've got to speak up a bit, like this.
Penny for the Guy!
Penny for the Guy!
Thank you mister.

Sam: (*Quieter*) Penny for the Guy.

Jo: Louder!

Sam: (*Louder*) Penny for the Guy!
Cor... thanks!

Jo: That's it, brilliant! Penny for the Guy!

Scene 3

(The Garden Shed.)

Sam: D'you think he'll be all right in here?

Jo: Yeah, of course. It's only for an hour or so.

(They leave.)

Guy: (*Thinking aloud*) I wonder what will happen to me after that day of torture. Being paraded in the streets for people to throw things... I suppose eventually those guards will return. And take me to the gallows...
I wonder what happened to the others, Catesby, Tresham and the rest. I hope they are still at liberty...

Peter Cansell

Preparing a performance

In your groups of three, prepare to do a performance of the extract as though it were a radio play. In other words, you will act it out, reading from the script. This is what happens in a radio play performance, rather than acting it from memory.

As you rehearse, pay attention to the following and look carefully at the highlighted sections of the script.

■ **Characters**
What are Sam and Jo like? How old do you think they are? Are they like people you know? Can you notice any differences between them?
How will you make Guy different from Sam and Jo in your performance? What should his voice sound like?

■ **Dialogue**
How will you make the dialogue sound realistic? Notice how Guy's language is different from Sam's and Jo's.

■ **Action**
In a stage play, the audience needs to see what happens; in a radio play, they need to hear what happens. Which parts of the extract need 'sound effects' in order to make them work? Which of those can you produce easily in the classroom (and which ones will you need to 'collect' out of school)?

Comparing performances

1 First, get together with another group and take it in turns to perform the extract as a radio play. Discuss the two performances. (Which parts were particularly successful? Were there any especially good ideas?)

2 Then watch the video of another group of students who have rehearsed the same scene and are now performing it. (It will be a good idea to view it more than once.) In your groups, discuss which parts of the video performance were:

■ different from yours
■ especially successful or interesting

In particular look at the highlighted sections of the script on pages 126–127 and decide what the students on the video did at those points, in order to make the characters, dialogue, and action come alive.

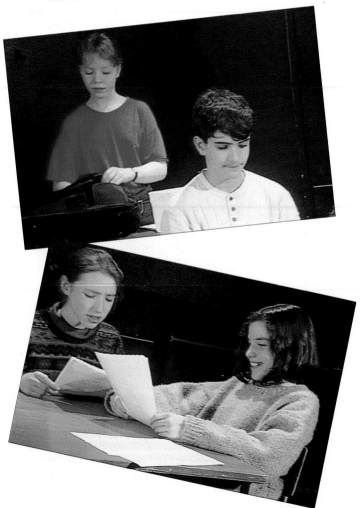

Completing the play

This is how *Guy's Thoughts* ends. In your original groups, complete your radio play by rehearsing and performing this final sequence. Try to use what you have learned from your earlier rehearsals and discussions.

Remember to think again about:

Characters Is there anything new that we learn about the characters in this final part of the play?

Dialogue You will need to think carefully about the best way in which to do Guy's long speech.

Action How will you give the impression of the guy being picked up? What about the sound of the fire? (Tissue paper being crushed can sound quite effective. Do you need to represent the sound at all?)

When you have finished, compare your performance of the rest of the play with the one on the video. What were you particularly pleased with in your version?

Guy's Thoughts

Part 2 Scene 3 (contd.)

Guy: ...If only my hand had not been stayed... if I had lit that fuse, things would have been so different. I might have died... but we should have won a great victory...

Perhaps I shall escape, no I'm sure I shall escape. Catesby will come and release me. I'll wager he's working his way in even as I rest here. He's brilliant, like a general in the way he plans things. He'll come... He'll come... Tomorrow's a new day, perhaps the rest have successfully started the rebellion...

Perhaps they will begin on the morrow having rid us of this shameful parliament... It may be that we will all rise up with the dawn and bring down the evil powers that control our lives. Yes, yes.

Now to sleep, tomorrow shall be a magnificent day.

(*The Guy falls over and goes to sleep.*)

Scene 4

(*The Garden Shed and Outside.*)

(*The door opens.*)

Sam: Hey, look Jo, he's gone to sleep (*Giggles*).
Jo: It's just fallen over, that's all.
Sam: (*Still giggling*) Shall we wake him up?
Jo: No, just pick him up and carry him.
Sam: All right grumpy, it's not my fault that you had to get your dad to buy the fireworks, we still got them, didn't we?

(They gather up the Guy who speaks in a voice unheard by the children.)

Guy: So soon? Wait!... Wait!... Don't you see?... There will be a new dawn on the morrow...

Sam: Careful you don't knock his hat off.

Jo: Never mind his hat, his head is coming off!... Or more likely he'll be split down the middle the way you're pulling, hang on.

Guy: No!... No!... Not yet, Catesby will arrive with the new day. Wait, you don't understand.

Sam: How are we going to make sure he stays in one place?

Jo: Tie him to that pole sticking out of the top.

Guy: No... Wait!... You will be saved too, if we can only overturn this wicked government... won't you wait?

Sam: How's that?

Jo: Fine. I wonder if he'll burn...

Guy: *(Wailing)* No, no, no... You don't understand... Catesby!...

Sam: Wow! Look at that blaze!

Jo: Brilliant. That's what Bonfire Night is really all about.

Peter Cansell

Discussing the play

1 What do you actually know about Guy Fawkes? Share your knowledge as a class and then discuss how the writer of *Guy's Thoughts* has used historical facts in his play.

2 The play ends with Jo saying: 'That's what Bonfire Night is really all about.' Bearing in mind the rest of the play, what do you think when you hear that final line?

Shaping the Play
Making decisions

In deciding how best to perform *Guy's Thoughts*, you had to make a number of important decisions (for example, about how Guy should speak, or how to represent the sound of the fire – even if it needed to be represented at all).

In this next extract we meet Shakespeare's six workmen again. They have met in the wood at night, as arranged, and are about to face similar decisions about their play.

First read the scene in groups of four (Snug and Flute are silent).

A Midsummer Night's Dream

Act 3 Scene 1

(*Enter* **Quince, Snug, Bottom, Flute, Snout,** *and* **Starveling**.)

Bottom: Are we all met?

Quince: Pat, pat; and here's a marvellous convenient place for our rehearsal. This green plot shall be our stage, this hawthorn-brake our tiring house, and we will do it in action, as we will do it before the duke.

Bottom: Peter Quince!

Quince: What sayest thou, bully Bottom?

Bottom: There are things in this comedy of Pyramus and Thisbe that will never please. First, Pyramus must draw a sword to kill himself, which the ladies cannot abide. How answer you that?

10 **Snout:** By 'r lakin, a parlous fear!

Starveling: I believe we must leave the killing out, when all is done.

Bottom: Not a whit, I have a device to make all well. Write me a prologue, and let the prologue seem to say, we will do no harm with our swords, and that Pyramus is not killed indeed; and, for the more better assurance, tell them that I, Pyramus, am not Pyramus, but Bottom the weaver. This will put them out of fear.

Quince: Well, we will have such a prologue, and it shall be written in eight and six.

Bottom: No, make it two more; let it be written in eight and eight.

20 **Snout:** Will not the ladies be afeard of the lion?

Starveling: I fear it, I promise you.

Bottom: Masters, you ought to consider with yourselves. To bring in – God shield us – a lion among ladies, is a most dreadful thing; for there is not a more fearful wild-fowl than your lion living; and we ought to look to it.

Snout: Therefore another prologue must tell he is not a lion.

Bottom: Nay, you must name his name, and half his face must be seen through his lion's neck, and he himself must speak through, saying thus, or to the same defect: 'Ladies,' or 'Fair ladies, I would wish you,'
30   or 'I would request you,' or 'I would entreat you, not to fear, not to tremble. My life for yours: if you think I come hither as a lion, it were pity of my life. No, I am no such thing, I am a man as other men are'; and there indeed let him name his name, and tell them plainly he is Snug the joiner.

Quince: Well, it shall be so. But there is two hard things: that is, to bring the moonlight into a chamber; for you know, Pyramus and Thisbe meet by moonlight.

Snout: Doth the moon shine that night we play our play?

Bottom: A calendar, a calendar! Look in the almanac; find out moonshine,
40   find out moonshine.

Quince: Yes, it doth shine that night.

Bottom: Why then may you leave a casement of the great chamber window, where we play, open, and the moon may shine in at the casement.

Quince: Ay, or else one must come in with a bush of thorns and a lantern, and say he come to disfigure, or to present, the person of Moonshine. Then, there is another thing: we must have a wall in the great chamber, for Pyramus and Thisbe, says the story, did talk through the chink of a wall.

Snout: You can never bring in a wall. What say you, Bottom?

50 **Bottom:** Some man or other must present Wall: and let him have some plaster, or some loam, or some roughcast about him, to signify wall; and let him hold his fingers thus, and through that cranny shall Pyramus and Thisbe whisper.

Quince: If that may be, then all is well. Come, sit down, every mother's son, and rehearse your parts. Pyramus, you begin. When you have spoken your speech, enter into that brake; and so every one according to his cue.

(Act 3 Scene 1 Lines 1–57)

William Shakespeare

Solving problems

In the scene, the workmen come up with four 'problems', as they see them. Bottom raises the first; Snout the second; and Quince himself is worried about the third and fourth.

1 In pairs, look back at the script and note down:
   - what each 'problem' was
   - what solution was finally agreed upon in each case

2 Do you notice any similarities with the decisions that you had to make for your performance of *Guy's Thoughts*?

In fact, if Peter Quince and his friends knew a little more about plays, they would realize that not one of these four 'problems' is a problem at all. For example, no audience would be frightened by a stage lion.

Taking it further

Write a helpful letter to Francis Flute, explaining why Peter Quince does not need to worry about each of the four 'problems' and suggesting what Flute might say to his five workmates to ease their worries. (Do not use the solutions that characters in the scene actually come up with: think up your own ideas.)

Then improvise a short scene in which each of the problems is raised and Flute explains what the sensible solutions are.

Writing and Performing

Setting Out a Script

The way in which a playscript is set out means that a playwright can provide a lot of information to help the people reading or rehearsing the play to understand it more easily and to perform it.

Putting it into words

In pairs, read the following piece of writing. It is the opening of a written version of an improvisation that a group of Year 7 students did, based upon one of the cartoons on page 118. One of the group has simply played back the recording of the improvisation and written down what everybody said.

In its present form, this is hard to read as a play, and the group who had done the improvisation would not be able to rehearse from it very easily.

I can't seem to find Mr Blenkinsop. Oh, er... He's gone out for a bit, sir. What do you mean, gone out for a bit? Well... gone out. But he asked me to see him here at three o'clock. And why are you people doing an experiment without a teacher in the lab? You know the rules. We, er... Ah, well, there is a teacher in the lab, sir... Sssh! What do you mean? Er, she means that you're here, sir. I know I'm here. And you know perfectly well what I mean. So don't get funny with me, Mason. (He goes towards Mason and they all try to block his view of the flask.) No, sir. Sorry, sir. I meant Mr Blenkinsop got sort of tied up, sir. Tied up? Yes, sir. Said he had urgent business somewhere, sir.

Looking at the layout

Look at the extract on page 135 – another scene from *The Turbulent Term of Tyke Tyler* (which you first met on page 120).

1   In pairs, look carefully at the ways in which a playscript is laid out.
    What is there about the layout which helps the actor or reader to tell:

- who is speaking
- when one character has stopped speaking and another one begins
- what the characters are doing while they are speaking or between speeches?

    The notes around the extract will help you to identify the main features of script layout.

2   In groups of six, read the extract again and then act it out. Pay particular attention to the help given to you as actors, by the information in brackets.

3   Now turn the 'Mr Blenkinsop' piece above into a playscript. (Assume that it is Mason who is replying each time, except when a girl says: 'Ah, well, there is a teacher in the lab, sir.' and the whole class goes: 'Sssh!'.)
    Are there any points in your script where you need 'extra information', like the words printed in brackets in the *Tyke Tyler* extract?

Tyke Tyler

(The class have just been informed by the Head that ten pounds has gone missing from a teacher's purse and that they will not be allowed home until a check has been carried out.)

The character's name is printed on the left-hand side before each speech

Kneeshaw: Don't see why we should stay in. 'Tisn't fair.

Simms: Betcha it was someone in her own class. How could it be one of us?

Linda: My Mum says it's a temptation to others to leave your money lying about.

Often the writing will give an idea of how the words are to be spoken

Kneeshaw: Your Mum is an old boot.

Sir: Quiet please and get back to your work. This is all we needed.

*(The class settles down. **Danny** is colouring a bird with a blue felt-tip pen.)*

You do not use speech marks (see page 152) in a playscript

Tyke: What's that? A kingfisher?

Danny: No, a robin.

Tyke: They're brown and red, twit.

Danny: I like it blue.

Tyke: (*Quieter*) It's okay. I got rid of it.

Danny: What? What you got rid of, Tyke?

stage directions (see page 137) show the things that are happening which are important to the story or how a character is saying something or behaving

*(**Tyke** moves as if to hit him.)*

Oh, yes. I know. The ten...

Tyke: Shut up, you half-wit!

Sir: Leave Danny alone. He was working well till you disturbed him, Tyke.

When they are in full sentences, they are written in the present tense

*(Child comes in with a note for **Sir** as buzzer rings. Class moves to go.)*

stage directions are not always in full sentences

Sit down! It's searching time. What a day! Let's start with the desks. This will take some time!

(Class groans. Lights dim.)

(Act 1 Scene 4)

Gene Kemp

Giving Helpful Information

As you saw in the *Tyke Tyler* extract on page 135, a playwright can provide information which will help the people reading or rehearsing the play to understand it more easily and perform it. On these pages you will learn more about this kind of information.

Discussing Frankenstein

1   In pairs, discuss what you know about the Frankenstein story. For example, what part does the character of Dr Frankenstein himself play? Who wrote the original novel? What connection do the actors, Boris Karloff and Robert De Niro, have with the story? How is the monster brought to life? Why does it all go wrong?...

2   Now read this paragraph from the beginning of Philip Pullman's adaptation of the story for the stage:

(**Frankenstein**'s room. It has high, arched windows through which can be seen mountains and forest. At the moment moonlight is shining through. The light is dim and flickers as clouds pass in front of the moon. Sinister music plays. Then a hand reaches down from above, as if from the roof, and pulls the window open from the outside. A second later the shape of a man – **Frankenstein** – is seen to climb athletically down the outside and in through the window. He brings with him a wire which seems to be attached to something up on the roof.)

(Act 1)

Predicting what happens

Decide what you can predict from this paragraph of information and, using what you may already know about the story, work out the answers to these questions with your partner:

1 What has Frankenstein been doing on the roof and what is he about to do with the wire? (What is the significance of the distant clouds?)

2 Where is the story set? (What sort of building are we in? What kind of countryside surrounds it?)

Information in stage directions

Most playwrights provide paragraphs of information of this kind. Because they help the actors and director to know how to perform the play, they are called **stage directions**.

There are three kinds of stage directions.

■ Fairly long descriptions of the set that you find at the beginning of a scene,
e.g. from page 136:
(**Frankenstein**'s *room.*
It has high, arched windows…)

■ Information that tells us what is happening,
e.g. from page 135:
(**Danny** *is colouring a bird…*)

■ Information that tells us how a character says or does something,
e.g. from page 135:
(*Quieter*) It's OK…

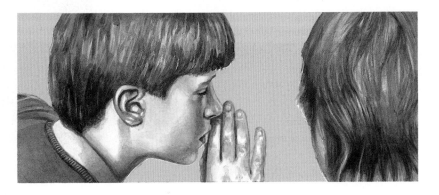

Set descriptions

1 To gain some idea of how helpful this first kind of stage direction can be, reread the set description on page 136. Then draw a rough sketch of the scene, as it might look when Frankenstein's hand reaches down to open the window.

2 When you have done that, in groups of four, compare your sketches and discuss any differences. For example, have you positioned the windows differently? Is the scenery outside different?

3 Decide which of these differences actually matter. In other words, how will they affect the way in which the play is actually performed?

Information about action and characters

Look back at *Guy's Thoughts* on pages 126 and 129. In pairs, pick out examples of these two kinds of stage direction (You should be able to find at least three examples of each.) Take each example and discuss which parts of the play would not have been clear, if it had been left out.

The language of stage directions

In pairs, look at each of these phrases from the stage directions:

> *It **has** high, arched windows…*
> *…moonlight **is shining** through…*
>
> *The light **is** dim… as clouds **pass** in front of the moon.*

As you learned on page 75, the highlighted words are known as verbs.

Verbs in stage directions are nearly always written in the **present tense**. In other words, they describe things as though they are happening or being seen now.

For example, these stage directions say:

> *It **has** high, arched windows…*,
> rather than *It **had**…*

Pick out the other verbs written in the present tense in the stage directions from *Frankenstein*.

(There is more about Verbs and Tenses on pages 146–147 of the Language Study unit)

Taking it further

Suppose that you were writing a play to be set in the room you are working in at this moment. Look at the room from one angle (you cannot show all four walls on stage!) Describe the main details as though you were writing stage directions. For example, you might begin your set description like this: *The English classroom. It has a large blackboard all along one wall...*

You could instead use the picture below as the basis for your stage directions.

Shakespeare and Stage Directions

Adding stage directions

Shakespeare did not include many stage directions at all when he wrote his plays. This means that when we act them, we have to decide for ourselves what the characters ought to be doing, or how they ought to be speaking their lines. The dialogue provides plenty of clues, of course. But mainly it is up to us to decide what should happen on stage to make the most of each scene.

In this third extract from *A Midsummer Night's Dream*, the workmen have finally arrived in the palace to perform their play in front of the Duke and the court.

Rehearse the scene in groups of six, in preparation for a performance in front of the class.

As you rehearse, you might find it useful to add brief stage directions on a separate piece of paper to some of your lines. (For example, what does Wall actually *do*, while speaking his lines? How does he behave while Duke Theseus and Demetrius are commenting on him?)

line 158: 'This loam...'
(He points to part of his costume.)

A Midsummer Night's Dream

[At this point, Peter Quince enters on the stage to deliver his 'prologue'
(a piece which comes before a play begins, to help explain what is going on).]

Act 5 Scene 1

(*Enter* **Quince** *as the Prologue.*)

Prologue: If we offend, it is with our good will.
  That you should think, we come not to offend,
110 But with good will. To show our simple skill,
  That is the true beginning of our end.
  Consider then, we come but in despite.
  We do not come, as minding to content you,
  Our true intent is. All for your delight,
  We are not here. That you should here repent you,
  The actors are at hand; and by their show,
  You shall know all, that you are like to know.
Theseus: This fellow doth not stand upon points.
Lysander: He hath rid his prologue like a rough colt; he knows not the
120 stop. A good moral, my lord: it is not enough to speak, but to speak true.
Hippolyta: Indeed he hath played on his prologue like a child on a
  recorder – a sound, but not in government.
Theseus: His speech was like a tangled chain; nothing impaired, but all
  disordered. Who is next?

(*Enter a trumpeter followed by* **Bottom** *as Pyramus,* **Flute** *as Thisbe,* **Snout** *as Wall,* **Starveling** *as Moonshine, and* **Snug** *as Lion.*)

Prologue: Gentles, perchance you wonder at this show,
But wonder on, till truth make all things plain.
This man is Pyramus, if you would know;
This beauteous lady Thisbe is, certain.
This man, with lime and rough-cast, doth present
130   Wall, that vile Wall which did these lovers sunder;
And through Wall's chink, poor souls, they are content
To whisper. At the which let no man wonder.
This man, with lantern, dog, and bush of thorn,
Presenteth Moonshine; for, if you will know,
By moonshine did these lovers think no scorn
To meet at Ninus' tomb, there, there to woo.
This grisly beast, which Lion hight by name,
The trusty Thisbe, coming first by night,
Did scare away, or rather did affright.
140   And, as she fled, her mantle she did fall,
Which Lion vile with bloody mouth did stain.
Anon comes Pyramus, sweet youth, and tall,
And finds his trusty Thisbe's mantle slain.
Whereat, with blade, with bloody blameful blade,
He bravely broached his boiling bloody breast.
And Thisbe, tarrying in mulberry shade,
His dagger drew, and died. For all the rest,
Let Lion, Moonshine, Wall, and lovers twain
At large discourse, while here they do remain.

(*Exeunt* **Quince**, **Bottom**, **Flute**, **Snug**, *and* **Starveling**.)

150 **Theseus:** I wonder if the lion shall be to speak.

Demetrius: No wonder, my lord: one lion may, when many asses do.

Snout: In this same interlude it doth befall

That I, one Snout by name, present a wall;

And such a wall, as I would have you think,

That had in it a crannied hole or chink,

Through which the lovers, Pyramus and Thisbe,

Did whisper often, very secretly.

This loam, this roughcast, and this stone doth show

That I am that same wall; the truth is so.

160 And this the cranny is, right and sinister,

Through which the fearful lovers are to whisper.

Theseus: Would you desire lime and hair to speak better?

Demetrius: It is the wittiest partition, that ever I heard discourse, my lord.

Theseus: Pyramus draws near the wall: silence!

Bottom: O grim-look'd night! O night with hue so black!

O night, which ever art when day is not!

O night! O night! Alack, alack, alack!

I fear my Thisbe's promise is forgot!

And thou, O wall! O sweet, O lovely wall!

170 That stand'st between her father's ground and mine;

Thou wall, O wall, O sweet and lovely wall!

Show me thy chink, to blink through with mine eyne!

(**Snout** *holds up his fingers.*)

Thanks, courteous wall: Jove shield thee well for this.
But what see I? No Thisbe do I see.
O wicked wall, through whom I see no bliss,
Curs'd be thy stones for thus deceiving me!

Theseus: The wall methinks, being sensible, should curse again.

Bottom: No in truth, sir, he should not. 'Deceiving me' is Thisbe's cue.
She is to enter now, and I am to spy her through the wall. You shall see,
180   it will fall pat as I told you. Yonder she comes.

(Enter **Flute**.)

Flute: O wall, full often hast thou heard my moans,
For parting my fair Pyramus and me:
My cherry lips have often kissed thy stones,
Thy stones with lime and hair knit up in thee.

Bottom: I see a voice; now will I to the chink,
To spy an I can hear my Thisbe's face.
Thisbe!

Flute: My love thou art, my love I think.

Bottom: Think what thou wilt, I am thy lover's grace,
190   And, like Limander, I am trusty still.

Flute: And I like Helen, till the Fates me kill.

Bottom: Not Shafalus to Procrus, was to you.

Flute: As Shafalus to Procrus, I to you.

Bottom: O, kiss me through the hole of this vile wall

Flute: I kiss the wall's hole, not your lips at all.

Bottom: Wilt thou at Ninny's tomb meet me straightway?

Flute: 'Tide life, 'tide death, I come without delay.

(*Exit* **Bottom** *and* **Flute**.)

Snout: Thus have I, Wall, my part discharged so;
And, being done, thus Wall away doth go.

(*Exit*.)

(Act 5 Scene 1 from line 108)

William Shakespeare

Taking it further

The three scenes from *A Midsummer Night's Dream* that appear on pages
122, 131 and 140 can actually be put together to make a complete play.
    In your groups, build on the improvisation you did with Scene 1 and
on your work on Scene 5 and rehearse for a performance of all three scenes.
    Think about the techniques that you have learned about in this module.
Work particularly hard on creating lively and interesting characters.

Choosing the Language

When making decisions about how characters in a play should speak, there are a number of choices that have to be made. They include:

Choice 1 Will characters speak in the 'natural', modern, day-to-day language that we hear around us all the time? Might it be better for them to speak in a different kind of English, such as the English that people spoke in earlier centuries, or in an imaginary 'alien-world' language?

Choice 2 Should the dialogue be in prose or verse?

(**Prose** simply means the style of writing or speech that we use normally in stories, letters articles etc. In other words, language which is not poetry.)

Playwrights' decisions

Think about the different choices that Gene Kemp, William Shakespeare, and Peter Cansell made when writing the plays featured in this module.

Using the options under Choice 1 and Choice 2, fill in a chart like the one below, adding entries for any other plays that you have read.

■ Notice that Peter Cansell and William Shakespeare made different choices for different scenes and characters.

■ If you are unsure about the choices that Shakespeare made when writing *A Midsummer Night's Dream*, read the opening sentence from the extract on page 140.

	Choice 1		Choice 2	
	Writing in the ordinary English of the time	Writing in an unusual English	Writing in prose	Writing in verse
Gene Kemp				
Peter Cansell (Jo's and Sam's language) (Guy's language)				
William Shakespeare (Acts I and III) (Act V)				
Other plays				

To choose day-to-day language or not?

Most people writing a play will choose to have the characters speaking in their ordinary, day-to-day language.

1 Shakespeare was no exception when he wrote
A Midsummer Night's Dream. When Snout says:
'Will not the ladies be afeard of the lion?',
he is speaking in the ordinary English of
Shakespeare's time (even though it sounds
strange to us today).

In pairs, find other examples of expressions
which sound strange to us because the
language has changed since Shakespeare's time.
Then turn to the Language Study unit on pages
154–155, where you can learn more about
Shakespeare's English.

2 Peter Cansell decided that although Sam and
Jo should speak ordinary modern English,
Guy ought to speak differently. His English
is more formal and 'old-fashioned', giving a
'flavour;' of what the original Guy Fawkes might
have sounded like in 1605:

e.g. 'There will be a new dawn on the morrow...'

Find other examples of Guy's speech, which
show how different it is from the way in which
Jo and Sam speak.

Choosing prose or verse?

Only one of the drama extracts in this module is written in verse: the
play that Peter Quince and his friends perform before the court in
A Midsummer Night's Dream:

'In this same interlude it doth befall
That I, one Snout by name, present a wall...'

Snout's speech, as Wall, is written in rhyming verse. In pairs, look back at
the script on pages 142 and discuss the rhymes in Wall's speech which are
not quite perfect ones and what you, as an actor, might do with them. (For
example, would you try to cover them up? Or might it be funnier to
emphasize them?)

Language Study
Verbs and Tenses

Three main verb tenses

On page 138 you learned that the verbs in stage directions are usually written in the **present tense**. They relate things as though they are happening now:

> e.g. ..*a hand* **reaches** *down... and* **pulls** *the window open...*

If we want to say that something has already happened, we use the **past tense**:

> e.g. ...He *told* us that his name *was*... Frankenstein. We *laid* him in my cabin and *looked* after him...

If something is going to happen, we use the **future tense**:

> e.g. ...I *'ll lead* you to the ends of the earth – I *'ll make* you *follow* me... It *will take* you as long as you live...

Tenses and playscripts

To see how these three different tenses can be used in a playscript, act out the following lines which come towards the end of Philip Pullman's stage adaptation of *Frankenstein*. You will need to be in a group of three.

Frankenstein

Frankenstein: Demon! Vile thing – destroyer!

Monster: Yes. Destroyer I shall be. I shall destroy you, my creator.

> (**Frankenstein** *leaps at him – but he avoids him, and taunts* **Frankenstein** *from the window.*)

Monster: You'll follow me, Frankenstein. Wherever I go you'll come stumbling after me, intent on putting me to death – but you won't catch me!

> (**Frankenstein** *runs at him again – and again fails to grasp the* **Monster**.)

I'll lead you to the ends of the earth – I'll make you follow me to the coldest, wildest, emptiest places in the world! I'll see you freeze and starve and suffer – and I'll laugh as you crawl through the barren mountains, the deserts, the ice-fields...

Frankenstein: I'll find you. However long it takes me, I'll follow you to the ends of the earth, and when I do, I'll tear you apart!

Monster: It'll take you as long as you live. Frankenstein, your sufferings are just beginning!

(He leaps through the window and vanishes. **Frankenstein** *kneels again and takes up the body of* **Elizabeth** *in his arms.)*

Frankenstein: What have I done? What have I done?

EPILOGUE

(Enter **Captain Walton.***)*

Captain Walton: So that was the story Frankenstein told me. When he came to the end, he fell back exhausted, near to death. I left him in the care of one of my men, and went out on deck to breathe the cold air and think for a while about the incredible things I'd heard. But I hadn't been there for long when there was a cry from below...

(Act 4 and Epilogue)

Philip Pullman

Looking at the tenses

1 Some of the verbs in this extract have been highlighted. In your groups, decide which tense each one is in.
2 What pattern do you notice in the way the future and past tenses are grouped here? What does that tell you about the way the story is being told in play form?
3 What happens next? Complete Captain Walton's account (using the past tense) in about a hundred words.

Accent

Different accents

You have probably noticed that many of the characters from the extracts featured on the video had different accents.

Accent is the name we give to the way in which people pronounce words when they speak. Our accent usually depends on the place where we were brought up, or the people we have spent most of our time with.

Identifying accents

1 In pairs, decide which accents the following characters have. Watch clips from these extracts on the video and listen to them carefully:

- Mrs Somers from *Tyke Tyler*
- Jo and Sam from *Guy's Thoughts*
- Roland from *Elidor*
- Jill Dando, the presenter from the BBC *Holiday* show

2 What is special about each character's pronunciation which enables you to say that they have a particular accent?

Listen especially to the following words and try to compare the way the character says them with the way you pronounce them yourself:

- Mrs Somers: staff, perfectly, along
- Jo and Sam: commuters, things, suppose
- Roland: towers, brother, my
- Jill Dando: swan, pounds, board

A neutral accent

You might have found it difficult to describe the accent of the voice in the BBC *Holiday* clip. She speaks in the 'neutral' accent that can be heard all over the country, and does not belong to one particular region. It is the 'standard' accent that foreign students learn when they are studying English; and it is known as **Received Pronunciation**.

1 To gain an idea of the wide range of accents heard every day, conduct a survey based on the voices you hear on television and radio. Draw up a chart like the one below.

2 When you have completed your survey (which could continue over a few days), pool all your data as a class and produce some statistics on 'The variety of accents heard on television and radio'.

You might choose to look into the statistics and answer questions such as:

- Is there one accent which is heard more frequently than any other?
- How often do we hear the local accent from our region?
- Which accents do News reporters most frequently use?

This work could be done most effectively by entering all your results onto a database.

Name of character/personality	Programme	Accent
Gary Lineker	'Sportsnight'	Leicestershire
Carol Smillie	'Holiday'	Lothian

Apostrophes

Two important uses

Look at these phrases from the *Frankenstein* extract on pages 146–147:

> e.g You won't catch me...
> I'll lead you...
> It'll take you...
> the incredible things I'd heard...
> I hadn't been there...

Each one of them contains a particular punctuation mark: the **apostrophe**.
The apostrophe has two quite different uses.

Using apostrophes to shorten words

1 In the example phrases given above, the job of the apostrophe was to show that a letter (or more than one letter) had been missed out.

> e.g. *I'll* is short for *I will.*

Look at each of the other phrases and write down what they would look like if they were written in full, without the apostrophes.

2 The apostrophe is a very useful punctuation mark in dialogue. Whether we are writing a play or a story, we want to show how the characters would actually speak. The monster in Frankenstein does not say 'I will lead you', but 'I'll lead you', which sounds much more like natural speech.
Here are three more examples from the extract from *The Turbulent Term of Tyke Tyler* on page 135, where the apostrophe has been used to make the dialogue sound natural:

> *What's* that?
> *They're* brown and red...
> *It's* okay...

Again write down what they would look like if they were written in full, without the apostrophes.

3 When Tyke says 'It's okay' we are seeing one of the most common uses of the apostrophe: to shorten *It is* to *It's.*
Notice, though, that there is a word which sounds exactly the same, but does not have an apostrophe: *its*, which means 'belonging to it' (as in the sentence 'The dog left *its* kennel.').

The apostrophe to show possession

In the title *Guy's Thoughts* the apostrophe is used for a quite different purpose: to show possession or ownership. In that title, the apostrophe is used to tell the reader that the thoughts 'belong to' Guy.

The rules for using the apostrophe to show possession are as follows.

1 When there is one 'owner' (e.g. Guy, Frankenstein, the monster), the apostrophe goes after the owner and before the 's':

    e.g. Guy*'s* thoughts
            Frankenstein*'s* room
            the monster*'s* revenge

2 When there is more than one owner and the word ends in a single 's' (e.g. infants, horses, parents), the apostrophe goes after the 's':

    e.g. the infant*s'* classroom
            the sound of horse*s'* hooves
            my parent*s'* house

3 When there is more than one owner, but the word does not end in an 's' (e.g. children, women, sheep) you add an apostrophe and then an 's':

    e.g. children*'s* books
            the Women*'s* Final
            sheep*'s* eyes

What is it used for?

In pairs, find other examples of the apostrophe in this book.

1 Decide in each case whether the apostrophe is being used to shorten words or to show possession.

2 If it is to shorten words, what would they look like written out in full?

3 Check with your teacher that you are certain about the rule for using the apostrophe to show possession and then discuss each example that you have found with your partner.

Punctuating Dialogue
Comparing playscript with fiction

Look back at the extract from *The Turbulent Term of Tyke Tyler* on page 135. At that point you looked at how to set out dialogue in a playscript. As you probably know, the rules are slightly different when we are writing a story.

Gene Kemp first wrote *The Turbulent Term of Tyke Tyler* as a novel, and then adapted the novel into a script to be acted.

1 Here is her original novel version of the episode which you met as a playscript. Read the extract with a partner.

Tyke Tyler

Each new speech begins with...

You need a new paragraph every time you...

And in no time at all I was back in the classroom, leaning over Danny who was colouring a bird with a blue felt pen.

'What's that? A kingfisher?'

'No, a robin.'

'They're brown and red, twit.'

'I like it blue.'

I bent nearer and lowered my voice.

'It's O.K. I got rid of it.'

'What? What you got rid of, Tyke?'

I went to hit him, but then a look came over his face like Leonardo with a new invention, or Einstein solving a problem.

'Oh, yes. I know. The ten...'

'Shut up, you half-wit!'

Sir looked up.

'Leave Danny alone. He was working well till you disturbed him...'

All the words actually spoken are placed inside...

The punctuation marks at the end of a piece of dialogue always come inside...

You also need a new paragraph when...

A speech will always end with one of four punctuation marks: 1...; 2...; 3...; 4...

Gene Kemp

2 Some unfinished notes have been written around the novel version, explaining the rules for setting out dialogue in a story. In pairs, complete each one and discuss the example of the rule in the extract. If you need help, look at the list of phrases below. They can be used to complete the notes on page 152, but you will need to decide which ending goes with which note.

3 With your partner, compare the two versions – novel and playscript – and discuss the ways in which each form sets out dialogue. You may need to look back at the notes on the layout of a playscript on page 135.

... a capital letter
... change speaker
... a comma, a full stop, a question mark or an exclamation mark
... the inverted commas
... inverted commas
... the dialogue ends

Inverted commas

Inverted commas, used in the punctuation of dialogue, are also known as speech marks or quotation marks. When we write by hand, we usually use double inverted commas:

e.g. *"What's that? A kingfisher?"*

Printed books normally use single inverted commas:

e.g. 'No, a robin.'

Taking it further

1 Turn back to the first extract that you read from *The Turbulent Term of Tyke Tyler* on page 120.
How would it have looked when Gene Kemp first wrote it as a novel? Turn the playscript into a section of novel dialogue, bearing in mind all the rules that you have learnt about. (If you have a copy of the novel in your school, compare your version with Gene Kemp's original.)

2 In pairs, improvise a few seconds of dialogue between Tyke and Danny or Tyke and Sir (about three sentences from each person) following on from the scene on page 152.
Write down the dialogue, first in playscript form, then as it would look in a novel. In the second, include phrases such as 'he said', but do not add anything else to the dialogue itself.

How the Language has Changed

The 'evolution' of words

Just as animals have evolved through time, so words have changed their meanings. And, like animals, some words have simply become extinct.

Each of the words and expressions in these cartoons is to be found in the extracts from *A Midsummer Night's Dream*, that appear in the Drama module. This is a play which Shakespeare wrote four hundred years ago.

'Extinct' words

Which of the underlined words do we never hear used these days? Write down the words or phrases that we would say instead.

'Evolved' words

Which of the underlined words are still in use, but have new meanings? What do you think the word meant in Shakespeare's time, and what does it mean nowadays?

From Act 1, Scene 2

...according to the <u>scrip</u>.

... you may speak as <u>small</u> as you will.

And, I hope, here is a play <u>fitted</u>.

<u>Pray you</u>... give it me...

...<u>con</u> them by tomorrow night...

Taking it further

You might have noticed in your reading that Shakespeare's verbs often have endings different from the ones we are used to today. Look back at lines 169–190 on pages 142–143. What does Shakespeare write instead of modern English 'you have', 'you are', 'you will' when a character is talking to one other person?

GLOSSARY

Accent   The way we pronounce words. Our accent usually depends upon where we were brought up, or the people we have spent most time with. See pages 148-149.

Adjective   A word which helps to give more information about a noun or pronoun, e.g. It was very *strange* weather. Yolanda was *beautiful, proud, haughty,* and *lazy.* See page 116.

Adverb   A word which gives us more information about a verb, e.g. *Suddenly* something fluttered to his shoulder. The black arrow sped *straight* from the string. See page 77.

Apostrophe   The punctuation mark (') which has two quite different uses:
1   to show that a letter or group of letters has been missed out, e.g. It*'s* all right. I*'ll* do it. We*'ve* finished.
2   to show possession (or ownership), e.g. *Guy's Thoughts, animals' faces.* See pages 150-151.

Audience   The name we give to the people we expect to read our writing or listen to what we say. It can also mean the people who watch a play or a film.

Autobiography   See **Biography**.

Biography and **Autobiography**   A biography is a book or article written about somebody's life. In an autobiography you write about *your own* life. See pages 106-109.

Borrowing   The English language has grown by borrowing words from other languages, e.g. Galaxy is borrowed from Ancient Greek; chimpanzee from Bantu, a West African language. See pages 78-79; also **Etymology**.

Character   A person in a story, play, or poem.

Comma   A punctuation mark (,) used to break up sentences and make them easier to understand, for example by separating items in a list or dividing up the different parts of the sentence. See pages 39-40.

Common noun   The general label we give to people, places, things or animals, e.g. sister, city, chair, owl. See page 74; also **Noun**.

Complex sentence   See **Sentence**.

Conjunction   A word used to join parts of a sentence, individual words or phrases, e.g. He waited *until* she had finished reading. See pages 114-115.

Coordinated sentence   See **Sentence**.

Dialect   A variety of language used by a particular group of people, which has its own words and expressions and its own set of grammatical rules. See pages 110-111; also: **Standard English dialect**.

Dialogue   Characters' spoken words in a story. See page 120; also pages 38 and 152-153.

Etymology   An account of the history of a particular word, including the language it came from and its original meaning, e.g. the etymology of 'biography' is two Ancient Greek words meaning 'life' and 'writing'.

Exclamation mark   The punctuation mark (!) used to end a sentence or a speech in a piece of dialogue if we want to show, for example, that a command has been given or something has been said urgently, e.g. 'Open it!' 'It's locked!' See pages 37-38.

Fiction   Writing which is about people and events which have been invented by the author, e.g. novels, such as *The Hobbit*, and short stories, such as *William's Version*.

Form   The kind of writing we are reading or producing, e.g. letter, poem, advertising leaflet, newspaper article.

Full stop   A punctuation mark (.) used to show the end of a sentence which is usually a statement, rather than a question or an exclamation. See page 37.

Grammar   The way words are put together or changed to make sentences. *Grammar* can also mean the 'rules' of a language or dialect.

Inverted commas   The punctuation marks (' ... ') used in the punctuation of speech. These are sometimes called quotation marks or speech marks. See pages 152-153.

Metaphor   A way of comparing things without using the words 'like' or 'as', e.g. My limbs are rods of steel. See pages 58-59.

Narrative   Writing or speaking which tells a story.

Non-fiction   Writing which is not stories, poems or plays, but deals mostly in facts, e.g. recipes, holiday brochures, encyclopedia articles. See Module 3.

Noun   The word in a sentence which labels a person, place, thing, feeling or idea, e.g. That is how *Nokomis* brought *rattlesnakes* into the *world*. Nouns can be **singular**, e.g. The *snake* raises its *head*. Or they can be **plural**, e.g. The *snakes* raise their *heads*. See pages 36 and 74; also **Proper noun** and **Common noun**.

Onomatopoeia   A word or phrase whose sound gives a kind of echo of its meaning, e.g. The *creaking* of the stair. See page 60.

Paragraph   A block of sentences linked by one overall idea or topic, e.g. the fifth paragraph of the 'Divers' article on page 87 contains four sentences, all about the medical condition of 'the bends'. See pages 112-113.

Parts of speech   See **Word class**.

Person   See **Verb**.

Personification   A special kind of **metaphor** in which an object or idea is described as though it were a person, e.g. Age's breath is short. See pages 56-57.

Plot   The series of events in a story and/or the way that these events are linked together. See pages 30-31.

Plural   See **Noun**.

Pronoun   A word which can be used in place of a noun to avoid unnecessary repetition, e.g. I, we, she, they.

Proper Noun   The label we give to a particular person, thing, place or animal, e.g. Batman, Africa, Roger Rabbit. Proper nouns always begin with a capital letter. See page 36.

Prose   Writing which is not poetry. See pages 144-145.

Punctuation   The marks we use in writing to make it easier to read and understand. See **Full stop**, **Question mark**, **Exclamation mark**, **Comma**, **Apostrophe**, and **Inverted commas**.

Purpose   The particular reason we have for writing or saying something, e.g. our purpose might be to persuade somebody, to give information, or to entertain them.

Question mark   The punctuation mark (?) used at the end of a sentence or a speech in dialogue to show that it is a question, e.g. Is that right? 'But what could we do?' What do you want? See pages 37-38; also pages 152-153.

Quotation marks   See **Inverted commas**.

Received Pronunciation   The 'neutral' or 'standard' accent that some people use instead of a regional accent. See page 149; also **Accent**.

Rhyme   Words rhyme when their endings have the same sounds, e.g. *Eyes, lies;* or similar sounds, e.g. *Matilda, killed her.*

Sentence   A group of words which makes sense. Sentences always begin with a capital letter and end with a full stop, question mark or exclamation mark. They usually contain a main verb. A **Simple sentence** says just one thing, e.g. Hamelin was plagued by rats. When we join two simple sentences with 'or', 'and' or 'but' we make a **coordinated sentence**, e.g. The Piper arrived *and* made an offer. When we use a different conjunction to show how the two parts of the sentence are connected in meaning, we make a **complex sentence**, e.g. The Piper took his revenge *because* the Mayor refused to pay him. See pages 114-115.

Simile   A way of comparing things in an unusual or unexpected way, in which the writer uses the words 'like' or 'as', e.g. a face *like* a map of the weather. See pages 58-59.

Simple sentence   See **Sentence**.

Singular   See **Noun**.

Speech marks   See **Inverted commas**.

Stage directions   Information in a play text provided by the playwright to help the reader or actor understand what is happening, what the set looks like, or how a character says or does something. See pages 136-137.

Standard English dialect   The dialect that is heard in any part of the country and is understood throughout the English-speaking world. Nearly all writing is in Standard English dialect. See pages 110-111.

Statement   See **Sentence**.

Tense   The form of the verb which tells us when something happens. Verbs can be in the **Present tense**, e.g. He *leaps* through the window. Or the **Past tense**, e.g. He *fell* back exhausted. Or the **Future tense**, e.g. I*'ll* find you. See pages 138; also pages 146-147.

Topic   The subject of a piece of writing or speech. The topics of extracts in this book include Divers, Shakespeare, and Holidays in Florida.

Verb   The word in a sentence which enables us to say what people or things are *doing*, e.g. Winter *crept* through the wood; or *being*, e.g. Spring *is* the winner! Verbs can be in the **First person**, e.g. *I* (or *we*) went out; the **Second person**, e.g. *You* left your coat behind; or the **Third person**, e.g. *She* (or *he, it* or *they*) came back. See pages 75-76; also **Tense**.

Word class   A group of words which do a particular job in a sentence, e.g. nouns label people, places, things, or ideas; pronouns take the place of nouns. They are sometimes called **Parts of speech**. The word classes dealt with in this book are nouns (proper nouns and common nouns), adjectives, verbs, adverbs, conjunctions, and pronouns.

Index of Authors and Extracts

Note: page numbers in italics refer to where texts are used in Language Study.

Acknowledgements

We are grateful for permission to reproduce the following copyright material:

Module 1 – Narrative
Kelly Bright: 'Who Am I?' collage, © Kelly Bright 1995, reproduced by permission of the author. **Linda Cotterill:** 'The Great Rain', first published in *Time for Telling*, ed: Mary Mendlicott (Kingfisher, 1991), reprinted by permission of the author. **Philippe Dupasquier:** extracts from *The Great Escape*, © 1988 Phillipe Dupasquier. Permission granted by Walker Books Ltd. **Alan Garner:** extract from *Elidor*, reprinted by permission of HarperCollins Publishers Limited. **Grace Hallworth:** extract from 'How Crab Got Its Back' from *Listen To This Story* (Methuen Children's Books), reprinted by permission of Reed Consumer Books. **Douglas Hill:** extract from *Planet of the Warlord* (Pan Books) reproduced by permission of Watson Little Ltd. **Anthony Horowitz:** extract from 'The Ten Fingers of Sedna', © Anthony Horowitz 1985, from *Myths and Legends* (Kingfisher, 1985), reprinted by permission of The Maggie Noach Literary Agency on behalf of the author. **Ted Hughes:** extracts from 'How the Elephant Became' and 'Why the Owl Behaves as He Does' from *How the Whale Became and Other Stories*, reprinted by permission of Faber & Faber Ltd. **Jan Mark:** 'The Wolf and Three Little Pigs' from *Nothing to be Afraid Of*, Copyright © Jan Mark, 1980. First published by Viking Children's Books, reproduced by permission of Penguin Books Ltd. **Catherine Storr:** extract from 'Huff Puff' from *Clever Polly and the Stupid Wolf*, reprinted by permission of Faber & Faber Ltd. **J R R Tolkien:** extract from *The Hobbit*, reprinted by permission of HarperCollins Publishers Ltd. **Rupert Widdicombe:** original chart 'The 12 Steps of the Hero's Journey' from *The Sunday Times*, 4 September 1994, © Times Newspapers/Supplements Limited 1994, reproduced by permission of Times Newspapers Limited. The chart has been adapted to include additional columns which did not appear in *The Sunday Times*.

Module 2 – Poetry
Hilaire Belloc: 'Matilda' from *Cautionary Tales* (Duckworth), reprinted by permission of the Peters Fraser & Dunlop Group Ltd. **James Berry:** 'Workings of the Wind' from *When I Dance*, Copyright © James Berry, 1988. First published by Hamish Hamilton Children's Books, reproduced by permission of Penguin Books Ltd. **David Calder:** 'Africa', © Dave Calder 1980, from *Continents* (Other, 1981), reprinted by permission of the author. **Roald Dahl:** 'Little Red Riding Hood and the Wolf', © Roald Dahl, 1992, from *Revolting Rhymes*, (Jonathan Cape, 1982/Penguin Books, 1984), reproduced by permission of Murray Pollinger. **Lawrence Ferlinghetti:** 'Johnny Nolan' from *A Coney Island of the Mind* (New Directions Publishing Corporation, 1958), reprinted by permission of Laurence Pollinger Ltd. **Pamela Gillilan:** 'Invasion' first published in *A Fifth Poetry Book*, ed: John Foster (OUP, 1985), reprinted by permission of the author. **Philip Gross:** 'Who Man' from *The All-Nite Cafe* by Philip Gross, reprinted by permission of Faber & Faber Ltd. **John Hegley:** 'I Need Contact Lenses', reprinted by permission of the Peters Fraser and Dunlop Group Ltd. **J A Hendon:** 'Sink Song', published in *Touchstones*, ed: Mike and Peter Benton (Hodder & Stoughton), reprinted by permission of Hodder Headline plc. **Simon Hobbs:** 'Grand Slam', © Simon Hobbs 1995, first published here by permission of the author. **Liz Lochhead:** 'George Square' from *Dreaming Frankenstein and Collected Poems* (Polygon, 1984), reprinted by permission of Polygon. **Roger McGough:** 'Winter Morning' from *Sky in the Pie*, (Puffin, 1985); ' The Sound Collector' from *Pillow Talk*, (Viking, 1990); and 'The Fight of the Year' from *You Tell Me* by Brian Patten and Roger McGough (Kestral, 1979), reprinted by permission of the Peters Fraser & Dunlop Group Ltd. **Adrian Mitchell:** 'Listening' from *The Thirteen Secrets of Poetry* (Simon & Schuster, 1993), © Adrian Mitchell 1993, reprinted by permission of Adrian Mitchell c/o Caroline Sheldon Literary Agency. **John Mole:** 'The Shoes' from *Catching the Spider*, Copyright © John Mole, 1992. First published by Blackie, reproduced by permission of Penguin Books Ltd. **Judith Nicholls:** 'Winter' from *Midnight Forest and Other Poems*, and 'Wordhunter's Collection' from *Magic Mirror and Other Poems for Children*, reprinted by permission of Faber & Faber Ltd. **Gareth Owen:** 'Song of the City' from *Song of the City* (1985) reprinted by permission of HarperCollins Publishers Limited. 'Ping Pong' from *Salford Road and Other Poems* (Young Lions, 1988), © Gareth Owen 1988, reproduced by permission of the author c/o Rogers, Coleridge & White Ltd, 20 Powis Mews, London W11 1JN. **Posy Simmonds:** illustrations for *Matilda* by Hilaire Belloc (Jonathan Cape, 1991), reproduced by permission of Random House UK on behalf of the estate of Posy Simmonds. **Judith Thurman:** 'Zebra' from *Flashlight and Other Poems*, Copyright © 1976 Judith Thurman, reprinted by permission of Marian Reiner for the author.

Module 3 – Non-Fiction
The Body Shop International plc: aromatherapy leaflet © 1992 The Body Shop International plc. **Book Marketing Limited:** statistical information from *Books and the Consumer 1994*. **British Airways Holidays:** extract from 1994 brochure on holidays in Florida. **Department of Transport:** extract from 'Drive' booklet produced to complement 1994 BBC TV series 'Drive'. **Helicon:** extracts from *The Hutchinson Encyclopedia 1995* (10th Edition), Copyright © Helicon Publishing 1994. **Hoseasons Holidays:** extract from 1994

'Boating in Britain' brochure. **Oxford University Press:** extract from *Oxford Children's Encyclopedia*, Volume 2. **J Sainsbury plc:** advertising material/'Simply Take' recipe card series. **Alan Sutton Publishing:** extracts by Michael Buerk and Laurie Lee from *I'll Never Forget the Day* ed: Bob Willey (Alan Sutton, 1988). **Usborne Publishing Ltd:** extract from *The Usborne Book of Bikes*, © 1990 Usborne Publishing Ltd. **A P Watt:** illustration/information page from *Almost Everything There is to Know* by Tim Hunkin (Pyramid, 1988).

Module 4 – Drama
Peter Cansell: 'Guy's Thoughts', © Peter Cansell 1995, first published here. **Faber & Faber Ltd:** extract from *The Turbulent Term of Tyke Tyler* by Gene Kemp (Faber, 1977). **Oxford University Press:** extract from Oxford Playscripts Series edition of *The Turbulent Term of Tyke Tyler* by Gene Kemp (OUP, 1990); extract from Oxford Playscripts Series edition by Philip Pullman of *Frankenstein* by Mary Shelley (OUP, 1990); extracts from Oxford School Shakespeare Series edition of *A Midsummer Night's Dream* by William Shakespeare edited by Roma Gill (OUP, 1981).

Although every effort has been made to trace and contact copyright holders prior to publication, this has not always been possible. If advised, the publishers will be pleased to rectify any errors or omissions at the earliest opportunity.

We would like to thank the following for permission to reproduce photographs:
J Allan Cash pp.53 (top left), 56, 57; **Edinburgh Photo Library** p.53 (top right, centre, bottom right); **Ronald Grant Archive** pp.30, 31, p.36; **Kobal Collection** pp.36, 136; **Life File** p.53 (bottom left); **Rex Features** pp.100, 148, 149; **Science Photo Library/Dr Gornacz** p.87; **Still Pictures** pp.108, 116. Additional photography by Chris Honeywell and Martin Sookias. Special thanks to Frideswide Middle School, Fitzharry's School, Sainsbury's plc, Lunn Poly and Kieran Boyle.

The illustrations are by:
James Alexander p.66, p.67, p.82 (top), pp.84/85; **Susan André** pp.106/107, p.110; **Rowan Barnes-Murphy** p.59, p.86, p.114; **Suzanne Carpenter** pp.48/49, p.50; **Tom Croft** p.120, p.135, p.137 (bottom), p.152; **Philippe Dupasquier** pp.8/9; **Jane Gedye** pp.24/25, p.37, p.63 p.76, p.96, p.121; **Valerie Hill** p.78, p.82, p.113, p.117, p.139; **Sue Hillwood-Harris** p.43, p.60; **John Ireland** p.94, p.95; **Gary Long** p.52, p.71; **Alan Marks** p.19, p.21, p.23, 38; **Sheila Moxley** pp.10/11, pp.12/13, p.61, p.79; **Colin MacNeil** p.26, pp.72/73, p.137 (top), p.138, p.150; **Felicity Roma-Bowers** p.14, p.15, p.62; **Linda Schwab** p.16, p.17, pp.40/41, p.54, p.55, p.70, p.75, pp.126/127, p.129, p.130, p.145, p.151 (top); **Posy Simmonds** p.44, p.45, p.46, p.47; **Duncan Storr** p.32, p.33, p.34, p.35; **Tracy Thompson** p.39, p.58, p.65, p.77; **Harry Venning** p.118, pp.154/155; **Stephen Wilkin** p.27, p.31, p.123, p.124, p.125, pp.131, p.132, p.141, p.142. Handwriting by **Kathy Baxendale**.

OXFORD
UNIVERSITY PRESS

Great Clarendon Street, Oxford OX2 6DP

Oxford University Press is a department of the University of Oxford.
It furthers the University's objective of excellence in research, scholarship, and education by publishing worldwide in

Oxford New York

Athens Auckland Bangkok Bogotá Buenos Aires Cape Town
Chennai Dar es Salaam Delhi Florence Hong Kong Istanbul Karachi
Kolkata Kuala Lumpur Madrid Melbourne Mexico City Mumbai
Nairobi Paris São Paulo Shanghai Singapore Taipei Tokyo Toronto Warsaw

with associated companies in Berlin Ibadan

Oxford is a registered trade mark of Oxford University Press
in the UK and in certain other countries

© Anne Powling, John O'Connor, Geoff Barton 1995
The moral rights of the authors have been asserted
Database right Oxford University Press (maker)

First published 1995
Reprinted 1996, 1997, 1999 (twice), 2000, 2001

ISBN 0 19 831190 7

Printed in Italy